PORTRAIT OF NEWPORT II

Text by Leonard J. Panaggio

175th Anniversary Publication
Bank of Newport

For Monique

on the occasion of
Bank of Newport's 175th,
and our 50th, anniversary.

Detail of late-18th-century map,
probably prepared for General
Lafayette, showing military establishments on Aquidneck Island.

— *Redwood Library*

Table of Contents

This old print depicts the landing in Newport of the French forces, on July 11, 1780. The army from overseas proved to be the strength needed by the hard-pressed Americans in winning the War for Independence.

— author's collection

Preface

When the original edition of *Portrait of Newport* was printed in 1969 for The Savings Bank of Newport, now the Bank of Newport, it was an exciting time for the city and Newport County's communities.

At that time it was written that a substantial part of Thames Street had been leveled for redevelopment projects. That has been done. The area offers fine restaurants, boutiques, art galleries and special-interest shops. We noted that an eight-story tower had been added to the Newport Hospital and that the Newport Bridge, New England's longest, was opened to traffic.

The Newport Public Library, a modern, climate-controlled resource for the city's inhabitants, replaced The People's Library, which for decades had been housed in one of Newport's first mansions. The new library has kept up with the progress made during this past quarter of a century — it offers all kinds of services, from a growing collection of famous motion pictures on video to use of computers by patrons.

Ground was broken on Goat Island for the city's first new hotel in a half century, and this was followed soon after by another in the cleared redevelopment area. Tourism was growing. Existing motels/hotels on the island didn't hesitate to erect additions, and several new facilities were built during the next 20 years. By 1993, Newport counted 50 bed-and-breakfast inns, several of which occupied mini-mansions and historic houses, as well as a room-for-rent in restored Rose Island Lighthouse in the middle of lower Narragansett Bay.

The Navy presence was strengthened by an expanding Naval War College during this period. Thousands of officer candidates were graduated as ensigns from their school, and Piers I and II were "home" for scores of naval ships — cruisers, destroyers, oilers, repair ships and hard-working tugboats assigned to the Cruiser Destroyer Force, Atlantic Fleet.

In 1969, with the publishing of a book containing documentary photos, prints and text, we asked ourselves "why did we look back?" We answered the question by suggesting that it is good for us to reflect upon the past. The city has been good to all generations who have lived here. Our people truly enjoy a quality of life, to use an almost-overworked contemporary cliché, with just about every type of sporting activity, unusual attractions, numerous historic shrines, gardens, cultural activities of a scale usually found only in larger cities, and the natural sea and land vistas of incomparable beauty.

Now we bring the book up to date. The portion covering the years 1819 to 1969 is reprinted just about word-for word, and text and illustrations have been added that review the past 25 years. It will now remind us of what has transpired, from 1819 to 1994, in this historic seaport city.

It is Bank of Newport's way of saluting Newport and Newport County communities, on the occasion of this — the Bank's 175th — birthday.

David P. Leys, *Chairman*   Peter S. Damon, *President & CEO*

Introduction

In June of 1819, a small group of Newporters decided to organize a savings bank. They held their first meeting on the 12th in the Old State House (now called the Colony House) and drafted a petition for a charter to present to the General Assembly. With the granting of a charter, the new corporation again met on July 24th to choose their officers and to arrange for the opening of the bank.

On August 21st, The Savings Bank of Newport (renamed the Bank of Newport, in 1987, and henceforth referred to by its new name) opened its first office at Two Pelham Street. Since that time, it has maintained a record of 175 years of service to the people of Newport County, the longest record of any savings bank in the state. In fact, the Bank of Newport is the seventh-oldest mutual savings bank in the United States.

Behind this record of accomplishment is a story. Two Pelham Street, back in 1819, was considered the ideal location for an enterprising new facility. The lower section of Pelham Street was in the heart of Newport's commercial and mercantile activity. Bannister's Wharf, now West Pelham Street, was one of the busiest wharfs in Newport. Packet ships and later, steamboats, utilized the wharf for the loading and unloading of cargo and passengers. Many shops were also located on the wharf, and that section of Thames Street was where you could find most of the sea captains of the town transacting business. Townsend's Coffee House, located on the northeast corner of Pelham and Thames Streets, was the best hotel in town. President John Quincy Adams stayed at Townsend's during his visit in 1826.

The 25th anniversary of the Bank, in 1844, was observed by moving to larger quarters. The Bank of Newport took over the Merchants Bank Building which, until the mid-1960s, stood at the corner of Thames Street and the former Government Landing.

"The Little Old Woman in Grey" is the popular name of the little house which stands on the south side of Pelham Street, just below the corner of Spring Street. It is diagonally opposite the house used as headquarters by the British General Richard Prescott. During the three-year occupation of Newport by forces of the Crown, it served as a guardhouse for Hessian soldiers. Built in 1771-72, it is one of several houses remaining on lower Pelham Street that stood at the time the Bank of Newport opened its first office in 1819. Around the time of the Bank's 150th anniversary, most of the 18th-century houses on the street were restored to their Colonial elegance.

— *Newport Historical Society*

The old Merchants Bank Building was the second office of The Savings Bank of Newport.

— *Newport Historical Society*

This building became insufficient for the growing business of the Bank and, in 1872, the Bank of Newport moved into its third building. A three-and-a-half-story brick structure, it had been built as an imposing private dwelling and converted to commercial use. It still stands at the corner of Thames and Green Streets and, for many years, has been the headquarters for the People's Credit Union.

The Bank of Newport occupied this building until 1930, when it built its main office on Washington Square. On Monday morning, August 25th, the treasurer of The Savings Bank of Newport, Harry C. Wilks, turned the key to open the big bronze doors of Rhode Island's newest bank building. Throughout that day, hundreds of visitors saw the huge new vaults and all the other new equipment and business machines which rated it as the ultra-modern banking house of the time.

Preparations for the Monday opening, a big task, had been accomplished over the weekend. A police escort guarded the valuable securities and other records as they were transported from the bank's former location.

The new building lived up to a contemporary description that said, "No expenses have been spared to give the building its true character of solidarity, combined with extreme beauty and grace, while it is equally true that nothing in the mechanical or technical end has been neglected." The beautiful structure of red brick, dominated by its tall and graceful marble columns, was a perfect addition to the classical architecture that could be seen in the other buildings around Washington Square. The new building complemented the Colony House; the then-Newport County Court House (now the Florence K. Murray Judicial Complex); the old Brick Market at the foot of the Square (now the Museum of Newport History); the unfortunately now-demolished Perry House which stood across the Square; and the Strand Theater (now the Jane Pickens Theater), a former church building which, in 1930, still retained its original column-dominated facade.

Newport's economic growth after World War II was due to the return of the city's lucrative tourist business (Newport is now referred to as "America's first resort") and the expansion and addition of facilities at the Naval Base (now the Naval Education and Training Center). That expansion eventually attracted industry, such as Raytheon's Portsmouth complex, and offices staffed by research technicians geared to the needs of a high-tech Navy.

The city's neighboring communities — Middletown, Portsmouth, Jamestown and Tiverton (with adjacent Little Compton), experienced population growth, along with commercial and housing development. The officers of the Bank of Newport, acceding to the banking needs of the county's communities, opened five branch offices within a 25-year period.

Middletown's branch office opened late in 1961 at Two Mile Corner, the hub of the community's growth. Next came the Tiverton office in 1963. The Portsmouth branch, which dominates that part of the town known as Cozy Corner, opened its doors in 1967. The Jamestown office went into operation in 1975. The first banking facility to accomodate residents of the southern section of Newport, the Wellington Square office, opened in 1986.

Bank of Newport's growth now required an administration building. That was erected

in 1979, adjacent to the Middletown office. With a new outlook came the name change to Bank of Newport, on June 1, 1987.

The words in a notice drafted by those far-seeing men of Newport, back in 1819 when they prayed that the General Assembly would grant them a charter, have as much meaning now as then. At their first meeting, on June 9, they invited "gentlemen who are favorably disposed to aid in the establishment of said institution," and further noted that "The beneficial effects of an institution of this kind, in offering inducement for frugality and indus-

Still standing at the corner of Thames and Green Streets is this structure which was the third office of the Bank.

— author's collection

9

try to the laboring classes of the community, are obvious, and have been already experienced in some sections of the country."

They were solid words, and several of Newport's leading citizens responded to form the new corporation. In the charter which was granted appears the following statement: "The object of the Institution is to promote a safe and profitable mode of enabling industrious persons of all descriptions to invest such parts of their earnings or property as they can conveniently spare, in a manner which will afford them profit and security."

It is a matter of record that, during the past 175 years, thousands of Newport County residents have utilized the facilities of the nation's seventh-oldest mutual savings bank for their "profit and security."

Bicyclists, Washington Street, 1884.
— *Newport Historical Society*

Acknowledgments

The famous Chinese proverb says, "One picture is worth more than 10,000 words." Perhaps the person who said that saw the picture during the time it was painted, and therefore had an advantage. Many of the pictures reproduced on these pages were made long before we were born. And so there was experienced the reverse of the ancient proverb: words were needed to describe the images, hundreds of which were researched for this Bank of Newport anniversary edition.

Many have assisted in seeking the words for the pictures and in searching for the pictures in files located at different places. I am deeply grateful for the assistance given to me. Mrs. Ralph Pyne of the Providence Public Library's Reference Department; Mrs. Laurence E. Tilley and Noel P. Conlon of the Rhode Island Historical Society staff; Stanley A. Ward, Mrs. Oliver W. Cushman and Mrs. Peter Bolhouse of the Newport Historical Society's staff, who were repeatedly called upon to verify much of the material — particularly Mrs. Bolhouse, whose knowledge of Newport County is known to many researchers and has earned her being designated as the first "Newport Historian." John T. Hopf did wonders in copying faded photographs so that they could be reproduced in this work. My wife also assisted in preparing the manuscript and searching for photographs. Thanks are due to the numerous artists and photographers whose works make up a considerable part of the documentary illustrations in this book.

Several individuals and organizations were consulted for source material. They are acknowledged in the proper places. Photos from the archives of *The Newport Daily News* are reproduced through the courtesy of Mrs. Edward A. Sherman, Sr. In many instances, pictures loaned by various interested parties are published for the first time, and therefore add much to this documentary publication of Newport and its neighboring communities.

My thanks for the privilege of producing this publication go to the officers and others associated, in various capacities, with the Bank of Newport.

L. J. P.

The house of Governor William Coddington, one of the original settlers of Portsmouth and Newport, once stood on Marlborough Street. This old woodcut was often used to illustrate articles about Newport during the last century.

— Providence Public Library

A small farmhouse in Middletown (then Newport) was improved and enlarged in 1729 by George Berkeley, who had come to America to establish a college in Bermuda. The great philosopher named it "Whitehall." Nearby, in the vicinity of the Hanging Rocks and Purgatory, he wrote some of his many works. When he came to Newport he was accompanied by John Smibert, the first professional artist in America.

Berkeley established the Philosophical Society of Newport, whose members continued the club after he returned to England two years later. The Philosophical Society established the roots of what became the Redwood Library Company. Berkeley, who was once Dean of Derry, became the Bishop of Cloyne.

— author's collection

All Around the Town

On April 30, 1639, Nicholas Easton and his son Peter left the settlement of Pocasset (now known as Portsmouth). In a crude boat, they rowed southward along the west shore of Aquidneck Island and landed on a small island which they named Coasters Harbour. The next day they explored that section of Aquidneck Island around which was established the present city of Newport.

The Eastons were joined by William Coddington and several other men who, on May 15, held the first meeting in Newport. William Dyer, the secretary or clerk of the new colony, recorded, "It is Agreed & ordered, that the Plantacon now begun att this South west end of the Island shall be called Newport."

The harbor side of the settlement was swampy, and it was almost decided that the new community should be established around the present Easton's or Newport Beach. However, no shipping could be conducted at this location; the group re-examined the harbor area and found it safe and satisfactory for the development of a port. The town would be built along the fringe of the swamp.

A spring of fresh water was found near the present corner of Spring and Touro Streets, and at the meeting of May 16, the last order of business was "It is ordered that the Towne shall be built up on both the sides of the spring & by the seaside Southward."

No time was wasted in planning for the growth of Rhode Island's third town. John Clarke, Robert Jeffreys and William Dyer were empowered "to lay out all the lands for the town's accomodation, as also all highways" on July 11. Thames Street was the first to be planned. Negotiations were made with local Indians for the swamp that edged the harbor to be filled in for the cost of colorful coats and buttons. Thames Street was laid out over this reclaimed area.

Other streets were soon developed, and by the early 1700s, wharves began jutting out into the harbor from which Newport ships sailed to distant ports. In 1739, work began on the construction of Long Wharf which was completed about two years later.

Thames Street became the principal artery of Newport and along this almost-true-north-south highway, most of the city's merchants opened their shops. Long Wharf, with other wharves, connected the city and its merchants with markets in the other

White Horse Tavern as it appeared in 1870. The building, which dates from the 1680s and is located on the corner of Marlborough and Farewell Streets, was used for meetings of the General Assembly and the Town Council. The side showing the strolling woman faces Liberty Park.

— *Preservation Society of Newport County*

colonies and the Caribbean. Newport ships were heavily committed to the "Triangle Trade" which saw the shipment of rum to Africa in exchange for slaves. The slaves were shipped to Caribbean ports, and there, traded for molasses which was brought to Newport and distilled into more rum.

Other streets developed to accommodate the growing town. There was a road to the beach, and of course a highway from the center for stages to carry passengers to Providence and Boston. The farmlands of the Bellevue Avenue area eventually disappeared as wealthy families from Boston, New York, Philadelphia and

It is hard to believe, today, but this pastoral scene was the King Farm, once located in the Harrison and Carroll Avenue section of the city.

— Redwood Library

Baltimore built summer cottages.

Around Newport other communities were being settled. Jamestown was incorporated October 30, 1678. Tiverton and Little Compton were part of Massachusetts until 1746, when the eastern boundary of Rhode Island was settled. Tiverton was incorporated by the Province of Massachusetts in 1694, and Little Compton, which was incorporated in 1682, was originally a part of Plymouth Colony. Both these towns were annexed to Newport County on February 17, 1746. Middletown, which took its name from its location in the middle of the island, was taken from Newport and incorporated June 16, 1743.

More than three and a half centuries have passed since Anne Hutchinson and her followers settled Portsmouth, the first of Newport County's communities. Through the generations that have followed, the country has experienced some profound changes. From farming, fishing and other early communal occupations, Newport rapidly grew into one of British North America's leading ports and became noted for its artists and craftsmen whose talents were influenced by an advanced cultural society. This society

Located at the southeast corner of Mill and Corne Streets is the home of Michel Felice Corne, an Italian who arrived in Salem in 1799. There he did fresco work and also painted scenes in homes of the affluent in Boston and Providence. He spent the last years of his life in Newport and according to legend was the first man to eat a tomato in America — and live!

— *Preservation Society of Newport County*

was the foundation upon which the resorts of Newport and Jamestown flourished. Newport, Portsmouth and Tiverton established textile mills early in the nineteenth century. Coal was mined in Portsmouth during most of the last century and into the first two decades of the present century. Tiverton maintained a thriving fishing industry throughout the last century, with huge fleets of boats that fished the Atlantic Coast for menhaden.

The United States Navy is no newcomer to Newport County. For generations, Naval vessels have sailed in and out of Narragansett Bay. During the Civil War, the United States Naval Academy was temporarily located in Newport. In 1869, the government established the Naval Torpedo Station on Goat Island; in 1883, the Naval Training Station (now the Naval Education and Training Center); and a year later, the Naval War College. The growth of the Naval installation during World War II, and for half a century after, became a decisive factor in

"Newport Harbour from the Blue Rocks," depicts the Washington Street area of the Point, looking south, as it appeared during the 18th century.

— *Newport Historical Society*

the development and welfare of the area.

Modern industry established itself on Aquidneck Island soon after World War I when the Weyerhaeuser Company developed what is believed to be the largest privately owned port on the Atlantic Coast for its lumber and wood products distribution center. Established in 1924, the sprawling complex, with its deep-water pier, was closed by the mid-1970s. During the 1950s, the Submarine Signal Division of Raytheon opened its first building, and through the years added several more where at one time 3,000 were employed. By March 1994, with a slight name change — Submarine Signal Directorate — and employing about 1,200, Portsmouth continued to be an important component of this high-tech organization.

The Melville Fuel and Net Depot, a unit of the Naval installation, was downsized during the 1970s. Here was born the

John P. Newell, a Newport artist who was working between 1850 and 1890, drew this illustration of what Newport looked like as viewed from Goat Island around 1750, although he erroneously dated the view as 1730, almost a full decade before the Colony House (left of center) was built. In the foreground is Fort George.

— *Redwood Library*

The Bull House, a portion of which was built during the founding year of Newport, 1639, stood until a fire destroyed it prior to World War I.

— *Providence Public Library*

The Overing House, on the West Main Road, Portsmouth, at the Middletown line, was the country house of the British General Richard Prescott. On July 9, 1777, Warren-born Colonel William Barton, with a force of about 40 men, executed one of the boldest and most hazardous raids recorded in the history of the Revolutionary War when Prescott was captured as a prisoner of war.

— *author's collection*

The Sheffield House, a mansion that once dominated the area at the head of Eisenhower Park, was moved in 1925 to the corner of Division and Touro Streets to become the Congregation Jeshuat Israel Community Center. On the site was built the Newport County Court House, now known as the Florence K. Murray Judicial Complex.

— *Providence Public Library*

It doesn't seem like too long ago to many Aquidneck Islanders that the section of West Main Road near Union Street, known as Redwood Farm, looked like this. The picture is 100 years old.

— *Redwood Library*

first PT-boat training facility (Motor Torpedo Boat), where John F. Kennedy and Medal of Honor-winner John D. Bulkeley learned the art of PT-boat warfare. In 1974, some of this land was transferred by purchase to the State's Port Authority and Economic Development Corp. Since that time, that prime area has been developed into a super-sized yacht marina. The complex contains a sailmaking company and firms that build and repair boats.

In 1974, Middletown's voters approved the development of Charity Farm. This led to the formation of the Aquidneck Island Development Corporation. Its mission was to attract clients to what was then defined as an industrial park. The Island communities contributed to the promotion of the park, which at this time is tenanted by firms dealing in management engineers, consulting engineers and computer-oriented services.

None of the above has changed the the complexion of the region too much. There are still a few flourishing farms, and the resort and tourist business continues to grow. Newport's streets become crowded when the world-famous jazz and folk festivals are held, or whenever a cruise ship makes a port visit. But, just a few miles away in Little Compton is another world of peace and beauty.

We wouldn't believe it unless someone told us, but this was the One Mile Corner, looking north on West Main Road, back in 1889.

— *Providence Public Library*

The Brick Market, built in 1762, (now the Museum of Newport History) originally had open stalls on the lower level which were used for the sale of meats and produce by various merchants. During the 1790s a theatre was established on the second floor. The building served as City Hall during part of the last century, and eventually became a hardware and novelty shop. It was restored, during the 1920s, through the generosity of John Nicholas Brown who gave the building to the City to preserve as one of the community's historic treasures.

— *Preservation Society of Newport County*

The Brick Market, 1915.
— *Preservation Society of Newport County*

The Perry Mill on Thames Street is one of the few reminders that Newport once had textile mills. It was built in 1835 by Alexander McGregor, a noted Scottish stonemason. This photo, taken during the early 1920s, shows the multiple uses of the building; it had ceased operation as a mill before the end of the 19th century. The occupants included a roller rink, a plumbing and heating contract engineer (Thomas B. Connolly), and the machine shop of Gilbert H. Burnham.

— *Newport Historical Society*

△ The east side of Thames Street is seen in this photograph, looking north in the vicinity of Mary Street. Gladding's Express office was in the rear of a building not shown. Otto L. Ruecker was the proprietor of the watchmaker's shop, over which hangs an ornamental sign.

— Preservation Society of Newport County

▽ Located at the corner of Thames Street and Cotton's Court was the bookshop of Charles E. Hammett, Jr., which he operated for more than half a century. The enterprising owner, seen standing in the doorway, also provided bookbinding service and sold pianos and sewing machines (photo probably taken around 1880).

— Newport Historical Society

A not-so-long-ago view of Thames Street, looking south from the head of Long Wharf. Taken in 1951 before redevelopment cleared away buildings on the right (west) side, there are other changes to be seen. The classic street lamps were later replaced, and the building on the left corner lost its top floor as the result of fire.

— *Rhode Island Historical Society Library*

▽ The west side of Thames Street during the 1880s, showing the plant of the *Newport Daily News* and the *Newport Journal* which stood in the vicinity opposite Cotton's Court. George O. Herrmann's clock and jewelry shop carried an ornate sign composed of a watch and spectacles.

— *Preservation Society of Newport County*

21

△ Arch Avenue, also known as the Archway, was on the west side of Thames Street and south of the Brick Market. Number 145 was the ladies furnishing shop of Miss Mollie B. Lappin, and Edward Griffith's fish and oyster market flanked the southern side of the arch. This picture was taken in 1889.

— Newport Historical Society

▽ During the last century, the firm of Swinburne, Peckham & Co. was one of the area's largest dealers in lumber, hardware, brick, and sawmill services. The building was demolished around 1913 to provide for an expansion and garden-like approach to Government Landing.

— Newport Historical Society

△ An unusual 1890s photo, taken on a slushy day, of the corner of Thames and Gidley Street. Slender utility poles and red-brick sidewalks disappeared long ago.

— *Preservation Society of Newport County*

▽ The head of Thames Street, 1881, showing Liberty Tree Park on the left. At right, the second house from the corner of Poplar Street was the home of William Ellery, signer of the Declaration of Independence. Unfortunately, the hand- some structure was demolished prior to 1920.

— *Rhode Island Historical Society Library*

△ This is what the south side of Market Square looked like around the turn of the century.

— *Preservation Society of Newport County*

▽ Not a scene of some Klondike rush town, but a view of Thames Street when it was being paved with the most durable surface it ever had. "Belgian blocks" were laid on the long, narrow thoroughfare in 1908, with the help of dozens of sidewalk superintendents. The sign over the second-from-right awning marks the location of "F.W. Woolworth & Co., 5 & 10 Cent Store."

— *Providence Public Library*

△ The big clock on the east side of Thames Street, just south of Mill Street, has been a familiar sight for generations. Photographed soon after the turn of the century, it is about the only recognizable object, today, since so many physical changes have been made in this cluster of buildings.

— *Newport Historical Society*

▽ Erastus Allan established his crockery and glass business in this house on the south side of the Brick Market, on Thames Street, around the time of the Civil War. The narrow public way, south of Allan's, was Whittier Avenue.

— *Preservation Society of Newport County*

The Perry Mansion Market capitalized upon the fact that the building was once the home of Commodore Oliver Hazard Perry, USN.

— Newport Historical Society

The wharfs of Newport were for a long time the fingers of trade, commerce, industry and tourism that spread out into the harbor and along the entire Thames Street waterfront. Thus many businesses and trades were conducted on the wharfs, as shown in this circa 1885 view of Commercial Wharf. In addition to the sign indicating a terminal for the Newport & Wickford Railroad and Steamboat Co., the Continental Steamboat Company's office was located here. Just left of center is the sailmaking loft of John F. Scott, and dominating the photo is the flour, hay and grain firm of Briggs & Co. The hackmen shown here are drumming up business from one of the "up river" steamboats which has just unloaded an excursion.

— Mrs. Salvatore L. Virgadamo

On summer evenings, the benches on Elm Street Pier would be occupied with residents of the Point, enjoying cool breezes off the bay (photograph was taken in 1885).

— *Providence Public Library*

Stone Bridge, from the Tiverton side, 1865.

— *Stone Bridge Inn*

In 1794, the Rhode Island Bridge Company was selling subscriptions to build a bridge to span the Sakonnet River, at Howland's Ferry, from Portsmouth to Tiverton. Promoted as an undertaking for the "public good, and private advantage," when it and succeeding spans were built, it provided the only highway link with the mainland until the Mount Hope Bridge was opened in 1929. This 1890s photograph, looking toward Tiverton, shows a trolley of the Newport & Fall River Street Railway Company. The Railway, to assure patronage of the line, helped develop Island Park as an amusement resort, prior to World War I.

—*Stone Bridge Inn*

△ Long Wharf, looking east toward the Colony House, in 1885. Many of Newport's famous boat builders were located in the small shops that can be seen on the left.

— Providence Public Library

▽ This view of Long Wharf, taken prior to 1900, shows fishing boats unloading their catch for immediate barreling and shipping to Boston and New York markets.

— Providence Public Library

Disaster Strikes

It was a blow that came from way down low, from the direction of the southeast, and it laid all of Southern New England out cold for weeks. It struck on the afternoon of September 21, 1938, and Rhode Island caught the full force of the punch. Without warning, a tropical hurricane rushed into the region and, within a few hours. claimed over 300 lives and did more than $100 million damage. Portsmouth counted 19 dead, and seven school children riding a bus in Jamestown were swept to their deaths, while elsewhere in Newport and the County another 26 lost their lives when a tidal wave dealt a coup de grâce to the exposed coast.

Hundreds of Newport area homes were washed away or damaged beyond repair. Thousands of beautiful big trees suc-

cumbed to the soaked earth and the 130-mile-per-hour wind. All County beaches were in ruins, and Newport's waterfront and the Thames Street-Long Wharf section was strewn with beached fishing boats and small pleasure craft. Lumber from lumber yards floated up into the streets. Great sections of Ocean Drive and Cliff Walk were inundated. Large excursion and freight steamers were torn from their docks and drifted into the harbor or up into the

Shown here is the Block Island excursion steamer, *Westport*, which had been at her dock, Pinniger & Manchester's Wharf, on the left. The tidal wave lifted her up and dumped her across the front of Hammett's Wharf, in front of the Post Office.

— author's collection

bay. Windows of stores were smashed by flying debris or from the force of the wind. Martial law was declared and National Guard troops moved in to prevent looting.

Countless of our County's people were homeless and sought assistance from the American Red Cross; aid and shelter was provided by many organizations. Communication with the outside was next to impossible, because hundreds of utility poles went down under the savagery of the storm. Drinking water had to

In this photograph, almost all of the cabana section of Bailey's Beach has been washed away. The main section of the club house was still being battered when a daring photographer took this picture. The building was moved far from its original foundation and destroyed.

— *Providence Public Library*

be boiled, because reservoirs had become polluted. When a final tabulation was made, it was determined that Newport alone suffered losses amounting to $5 million, one-fifth of it along the waterfront.

People

Although the towns that comprise Newport County were settled by people whose original homes were in England, the ancestry of our people today can be traced to almost every nation of the world. The pattern was set long before there was a permanent settlement in the region.

Historians record that the Portuguese navigator Miguel Cortereal was exploring Narragansett Bay in 1511. Giovanni da Verrazzano, on a mission of exploration for King Francis I of France, anchored his ship in Newport Harbor in 1524. The Italian navigator and his crew remained here for two weeks. In 1614, Captain Adriaen Block, of Holland, was in the vicinity, and his name was given to the island about 12 miles southwest of Newport.

Rhode Island was the New World's first haven for those whose religious beliefs conflicted with the doctrines of other settlements and nations. It was to the little colony that those who held to other faiths came. Roger Williams, founder of the State, had said, "I desire not that liberty to myself which I would not freely and impartially weigh out to all the consciences of the world besides. All these Consciences, yea, the very Consciences of the Papists, Jews, etc. . . ought freely and impartially to be permitted their several respective worships and what of maintaining them, they freely choose."

Newport had been established only 19 years when, in the spring of 1658, a small group of Sephardic Jews settled here. They introduced Free Masonry (three degrees), and the manufacture of sperm oil candles. By 1760, their economic and mercantile impact was profound. They were engaged in several enterprises, from operating distilleries and sugar refineries, to ropewalks and shipping. It was said that Aaron Lopez had about 30 ships engaged in world trade, and many more vessels that were used for the coasting business.

Slavery brought the first black people to the area. Although they bore the label of slaves, for the most part they were treated kindly by their masters. Many of the slaves, when they died, were buried in the family plots. A school for black children was established in Newport in 1763. It was located on High Street. In the *Newport Mercury* of Monday, March 28, 1774, Mrs. Mary Brett, who kept the school, informed the public "that the school for the

One of Rhode Island's leading black citizens, Rev. Mahlon Van Horne, served from 1868 until 1896 as the pastor of the Union Congregational Church, on Division Street. During this period he attained the distinction of serving several terms on the City's school committee and was elected to three annual terms as a representative of Newport to the General Assembly. Mr. Van Horne was born in Princeton, N.J., on March 5, 1840, and graduated from Lincoln University, 1868. He was appointed the United States Consul at St. Thomas in the Virgin Islands, then part of the Danish West Indies. He died May 25, 1910, at Graceland, Antigua, British West Indies.

Another facet of this talented man was his experimentation with the propagation of pond lilies. In 1893, while strolling among the gentle hills of Matunuck, he spotted a pond practically covered with the beautiful water flowers. Using an old door for a raft, he sculled about the pond and obtained several excellent roots. The plants withstood the shock of the transfer, and Mr. Van Horne raised the pond lilies in a cement tank he had in his house on John Street. By October, the leaves reached a diameter of 18 inches, and the snow-white blossoms attracted many people to see the results of his experiment.

— Newport Historical Society

instruction of NEGRO children gratis, is again opened to all societies."

The Chinese population of Newport, around the turn of this century, was 40. It grew large enough within a few years to require the opening a Chinese Sunday School.

From all parts of the world came the people who helped Newport County grow and flourish. The Irish, Italians and Portuguese came to work in the small textile mills, to farm and fish, or to labor on the construction of Fort Adams. Their skills were also used in the erection of the huge summer cottages for

President Ulysses S. Grant was in the first year of his first term when nine-year-old Antonio G. Ferretti left Genoa, Italy, and arrived in this country. When a young man, he became associated with his brother in the fruit business in Lynn, Massachusetts. In 1889, he came to Newport and soon opened a fruit and confectionery store under the name of Antonio G. Ferretti & Co. He specialized in foreign and domestic fruit, and his store became the destination for those who sought the best. He did a brisk business with the summer colony, and he soon opened a Bellevue Avenue branch. His enterprise as an accommodating merchant saw him establish the first motor vehicle delivery service in Newport. In 1949, he retired to Fort Lauderdale, Florida, where he died in 1950 at the age of 89.

The store shown here was located at the southwest corner of Thames Street and Bowen's Wharf. In this picture, Antonio G. Ferretti is standing at the left of the trio. The decorations indicate that the photo was taken in 1892, the 400th anniversary of the discovery of America by another Genoese, Christopher Columbus. Around 1900, the store was moved to the east side of the street, near the corner of Prospect Hill Street, and there it flourished until the business was sold.

— Newport Historical Society

which Newport became famous. That seafood delicacy, the lobster, satisfied many an appetite because of Newport's Greek colony, a hardy band of fishermen who dominated the Newport waterfront for many decades. Historic Trinity Church had among its founders a French Huguenot, Gabriel Bernon.

Our people include Tiverton-born Robert Gray, the first man to sail the American flag around the world. Some natives of Newport were Philip Mercer Rhinelander, the Episcopal Bishop of Pennsylvania; eminent geologist Clarence King, famed for his work in the Rockies; and Secretary of the Treasury Ogden Mills.

People of Newport have dug the gold of California, harpooned whales, served in diplomatic posts around the world, and have counted among them those who would give their lives for a cause. One was Mary Dyer, a Quaker, who defied Massachusetts and consequently was hanged in Boston in 1660. Buried in the

Holmes Burial Ground in Middletown is the Rev. Obadiah Holmes, a grandparent on the maternal side of Abraham Lincoln.

"This town is as remarkable for pritty women as Albany for ugly ones . . . ," so wrote Dr. Alexander Hamilton of Annapolis, Maryland, in 1744, while he was stopping in Newport on a tour of the northern colonies. We're glad that the young tourist made note of a fact that the men of Aquidneck Island and adjoining towns have known for generations. However, we're sure today's gentlemen would find Albany, too, has its share of beautiful young ladies.

The women who have been identified with Newport County — native, adopted citizen, summer resident — are indeed remarkable. It began in 1638 when Anne Hutchinson settled Portsmouth. She was the first of her sex to establish a town in America, and such an accomplishment would have assured her name and place in history. But she was a leader in another direction, that of religion. In 1638, in Boston, she conducted informal discussions in her home, emphasizing the covenant of grace as opposed to the covenant of works. For this she was cited as an antinomian. She was banished from the bay colony for "traducing the ministers and their ministry."

During the French occupation of Newport, 1780-81, many of the officers wrote of the charm, beauty and wit of the young ladies they met at social functions. One was the lovely Peggy Champlin, who attended a ball in honor of General George Washington. He chose her as his partner for a dance and asked her to select the tune. She named "A Successful Campaign" and it is said that the French officers took instruments from the musicians and played the selection as the couple stepped through the measures.

To name all the famous women who have been born, reared and lived in Newport County would be a book in itself. But we can name a few, one of whom was Julia Ward Howe, writer and poet, leader for suffrage, and author of the lyrics to the stirring "Battle Hymn of the Republic." Another is Charlotte Saunders Cushman, the first American actress to be given international recognition. She chose to build her retirement home in Newport, and in her own way was one of the first to make a contribution toward the establishment of the Newport Hospital.

Ida Lewis, the keeper of the Lime Rock Light, in lower

Peggy Champlin, George Washington's dancing partner.

— *Preservation Society of Newport County*

Ida Lewis, keeper of the Lime Rock Lighthouse.

— *Newport Historical Society*

Newport Harbor, became a heroine while still a teen-ager. She rescued many from squally waters and other calamities in the harbor, and for her bravery was the first woman to be given a medal by Congress.

In modern history, Newport will never forget the wedding, which took place in St. Mary's Church, of the young and radiantly beautiful Jacqueline Bouvier to the then United States Senator from Massachusetts, John F. Kennedy.

If the young Maryland visitor of 1744 were to return to Newport today, we are sure that he'd be "smitten and overwhelmed" with not only the beauty and charm of the area's women, but also by their talents and abilities which are revealed whenever a worthwhile project must be undertaken.

When the motion picture industry was in its infancy, the first studios were located in the New York area, with some enterprising young producers making films in New England locations. In 1913, "The Breakers" was a subject for a newsreel, and filming companies, actors and actresses were frequently seen in this area. This 1913 photograph may have been used for publicity in connection with a group filming sequences in Newport. The tall young actress with the Mary Pickford-style curls posed for her picture in front of the Opera House.

— *Newport Historical Society*

Unidentified Newport cabinet makers in their shop, circa 1890. Newport has long been noted for

Julia Ward Howe, author of "The Battle Hymn of the Republic," poet, philanthropist, lecturer and reformer. Born in New York in 1819, she died on October 17, 1910, in her 92nd year, at "Oak Glen," her summer home in Portsmouth.

Early in life she began writing, and by her frequent trips to Boston became acquainted with social, political and literary leaders of the area — Margaret Fuller, Horace Mann, Charles Sumner, Ralph Waldo Emerson — and Dr. Samuel G. Howe, whom she married in 1843.

Dr. Howe, a noted reformer and philanthropist, and his wife edited the *Boston Commonwealth*, a newspaper devoted to anti-slavery. She championed the cause for the emancipation of Negroes, founded the Woman's Peace Association, was one of the presiding officers of the Woman's Rights Congress that

met in Paris in 1878, and, among other organizations, was the co-founder of the famous literary Town and Country Club in Newport.

She was a Unitarian, but preached from the pulpits of several churches in Newport County. Mrs. Howe was the first of her sex to be elected to the American Academy of Arts and Sciences.

She was universally admired and respected. Only ten days before she died, she attended the induction of Rev. Marion Leroy Burton, D.D., as President of Smith College. Mrs. Howe was among those receiving honorary degrees. When she was taken to the platform in a wheelchair, where she was made a Doctor of Laws, the entire assembly of 3,000 gave her a standing ovation, and then, as if by magic, burst into singing "The Battle Hymn of the Republic."

— *author's collection*

its artisans and craftsmen, and today such shops as the John Stevens Shop, in business since 1705, continue the tradition that began in the early part of the 18th century.

— *Redwood Library*

James Gordon Bennett, Jr., deserves rightful recognition for his contribution to the development of Newport as "Queen of Resorts." The owner of the *New York Herald*, who managed, beyond comprehension, to run the business and be off in different parts of the world to cruise or vacation — almost at the same time — was responsible for the erection of the Newport Casino, the first recreation facility of its type in America.

Bennett introduced the game of polo to America in Newport on July 10, 1876. Bennett was the only one in a polo uniform; his teammates and opponents wore regular coach-driving costumes. Bennett advanced the sport of yachting by promoting a trans-Atlantic yacht race. He owned some of the biggest and most elaborate yachts of the time. He encouraged all forms of sports, and offered cups for balloon, airplane and automobile races. In 1872, he offered a $500 punch bowl for the winner of a yacht race from the Dumplings, off Jamestown, to a stake boat off Block Island.

He was regarded as one of the best "whips" among those who owned and drove four-in-hand coaches. He enjoyed Rhode Island clambakes, often cruising his yacht up Narragansett Bay with numerous guests to enjoy the traditional state feast at Rocky Point.

Bennett was a moody man and would fire someone on the spot at the slightest provocation. He could be generous. He thought nothing of providing a Christmas dinner for the 500 boys and 100 girls who sold newspapers in New York, or of donating, according to a report, $4,000 to the omnibus and stage drivers in Paris who were on strike in 1891.

He maintained apartments and villas in New York, Newport and France. For many years he leased some of the summer cottages, but in 1880 he purchased "Stone Villa" and enlarged the estate, which was conveniently located across the street from the Newport Casino. The next year each of the six gateposts were adorned with large bronze owls, the symbol of his newspaper. Here he entertained President Chester A. Arthur at one of the most fashionable balls ever held in Newport, on Wednesday evening, September 3, 1884. Two quartermasters from his yacht were stationed at the entrance, two more at the foot of the stairs leading to the second floor, and patrolling the grounds were at least 20 of the crew in their nattiest uniforms. A sergeant and eight Newport policemen were outside the grounds to maintain order among the huge crowd which had assembled to see the carriages arrive with members of high society, other VIPs and the President. Inside the house, 22 liveried servants were added to the force already engaged to operate the house. Every chef in town was sent to assist in preparing the collation, and waiters were in great demand.

Someone once wrote, "Mr. Bennett has revolutionized society at Newport. Once, everybody went stupidly and decorously up and down Bellevue Avenue every afternoon in the week. Now everybody varies this by going to pigeon matches, polo games, steeple chases, and four-in-hand breakfasts on stated days — all instituted by Mr. Bennett, who is not done yet."

— *John Hopf photograph*

An artist sets up his easel on the walk at Battery Park, Washington Street. His subject is the Naval training ship anchored only a few hundred feet off shore. In the distance, to the right of his umbrella, may be seen the lighthouse that once stood on Gull Rock.

This picture may have been taken around the early 1890s, and it may be presumed that the artist is Edward Mitchell Bannister, the foremost Black artist in New England. He was born in Nova Scotia, in 1828, and died in Providence, in 1901, where he had come to reside in 1870. He is considered the founder of the Providence Art Club (1880), an organization that may have been started in his studio.

Bannister considered the Point section of Newport a favorite place. One of his paintings, "Morning on the Point," now hangs in the African Art Museum, Washington, D.C. "Under the Oaks," a canvas he painted in 1875, won a medal at the 1876 Centennial Exposition in Philadelphia.

— *Providence Public Library*

Frederick W. S. Sprague was photographed around 1890 with a crowd that would follow him to listen to his discourses and theory that George Washington was the Messiah. He and his brother, Welcome, came from Block Island around 1860. According to various editions of Newport city directories, Sprague was a gardener. It is possible that the "S" in his name stood for Sinekay, and that it became pronounced as "Senaca," an appellation by which he was known most of his life. He once lived in a small house on Vicksburg Place, and later in a gaily decorated cart in which he went about, from place to place, selling tracts concerning local affairs and personages, and expounding his theories and prophecies. In this photo he may be uncovering the chart by which he explained his theories. Confusion exists to this day regarding the name of "Senaca" as there was a Senaca Sprague who lived on Spruce Street and died around 1906. Sprague died in January 1902.

— *Providence Public Library*

Presidential Visits

When President George Washington visited Newport in August, 1790, he began a succession of visits and vacations to this city by at least half of the nation's chief executives in office. It was his only visit to Newport as president, but he had made previous visits in 1756 and 1781.

Accompanying Washington was Secretary of State Thomas Jefferson, who became the third president. Included in the president's entourage was New York's Governor George Clinton who became Jefferson's vice president.

President James Monroe arrived in Newport aboard a revenue cutter on June 28, 1817, for a two-day visit. He was inspecting military and Naval establishments and therefore it was appropriate that the town's official greeter was Rhode Island Naval hero Commodore Oliver Hazard Perry. President Monroe called upon William Ellery, one of Rhode Island's two signers of the Declaration of Independence, and at that time one of the four living who had affixed their signatures to the historic document.

The steamboat service between Newport and New York often brought President John Quincy Adams to this town. On one occasion he inspected the new construction at the fort which was named for his father. Another time he toured Redwood Library. Once there was such a storm going on that the steamboat would not venture out of the harbor, and the nation's chief executive slept aboard the steamer while it was docked here.

President Andrew Jackson came to Newport on June 19, 1829, with a large entourage that included his vice president, Martin Van Buren, and, respectively, the secretaries of war and Navy, John H. Eaton and John Branch.

It was ten o'clock in the evening of July 5, 1847, when President James K. Polk arrived aboard the elegant steamboat *Bay State,* en route for New York. Despite the lateness of the hour, rockets were fired into the skies as the steamboat came into Newport Harbor, and salutes were fired by the Newport Artillery Company, Fort Adams and the revenue cutter *Jackson.* His stay was only for the period the steamer needed to unload and load cargo and passengers, but a huge crowd was on hand to hear him make a brief speech.

Three cabinet members were with President Millard Fillmore when he came to Newport on September 16, 1851. His family had been vacationing in the city since early August and he was reunited with them at a private dinner. The busy chief executive departed the next day, his family returning to Washington with him.

President Ulysses S. Grant made several extended visits to Newport during his eight years in office. His trips were made by New York steamer, the Wickford-to-Newport shuttle steamboat, by train from Boston, and once on the shakedown cruise of an ocean liner destined for service in the Pacific Ocean. One of his dinner hosts, in 1869, was summer colonist Levi P. Morton. Morton became vice president during the administration of Benjamin Harrison.

Late in June 1877, President Rutherford B. Hayes and his wife arrived in Newport, and one of the people he called upon was historian and diplomat George Bancroft, also a summer resident, who is best known as the founder of the United States Naval Academy. After the departure of the president, Mrs. Hayes remained in Newport to enjoy the hospitality of several of the summer colonists.

Chester A. Arthur was no stranger to Newport. He was an ardent salt-water fisherman — his favorite game fish being the striped bass which abound in our waters — and a member of the exclusive West Island Club in Little Compton, across the Sakonnet River. He was in Newport on several occasions as vice president, president, and, to use the term of that era, "ex-president." Although he was a favorite of Newport's elite summer set, and the honored guest at some of the most glittering receptions and dinners of the time, he often appeared in town without any fanfare. Once he was observed aboard the Wickford steamboat, enjoying the Narragansett Bay crossing, just like the other passengers. On another occasion he came into Newport riding on a farmer's wagon. Still another time he was seen walking down Thames Street, his tall form bending to avoid shop awnings, so as to prevent his hat from being knocked off his head.

On July 5, 1889, President Benjamin Harrison arrived aboard the cutter *Despatch*. The steamer was flying a huge president's flag when she was sighted off Brenton Point. While in Newport he

Chester A. Arthur (1830-1886), twenty-first president of the United States, frequently visited Newport.

— *Isabel D. H. Willard*

was shown the latest developments in torpedo manufacturing at the Naval Torpedo Station, and toured the Naval Training Station.

For several days during July 1893, President Grover Cleveland, another salt-water-fishing enthusiast, was cruising in Narragansett Bay aboard the yacht *Oneida*. Each evening, the yacht returned to an anchorage off Jamestown.

President Theodore Roosevelt was also a frequent visitor. He came as assistant secretary of the Navy, and on another occasion to attend the funeral of one of his band of "Rough Riders."

At 10:27 A.M., on Thursday, July 22, 1908, President Theodore Roosevelt arrived at the Naval Training Station to attend a secret meeting of the battleship board. It was one of several visits he made to Newport during his life.

In the lecture room of the Naval War College, the president decried the attitude of those who believe in a Navy for harbor defense only, saying that the defensive duties should be assumed by adequate fortifications, leaving the Navy totally free to go away in search of the enemy. "When it is necessary to hit," he declared, "be prepared to hit hard."

On Saturday night, August 23, 1902, he arrived in Newport to be one of the godfathers at the christening of the child of Mr. and Mrs. Winthrop Astor Chanler, at their residence, "Cliff Lawn." He was an overnight guest in the mansion and the next day the ceremony took place with the young child being given the first name of the president. Among the group present were Mrs. Julia Ward Howe, U.S. Senators Henry Cabot Lodge and George Peabody Wetmore, and the author of *The Virginians*, Owen Wister, who had a summer home in Saunderstown, R.I.

— *Newport Historical Society*

As president, he made a social visit to Newport to stand as godfather for the christening of Theodore Chanler. A few years later he attended a Naval conference at the Naval War College where he delivered an address advocating the need for a strong Navy.

The big presidential yacht, *Mayflower,* entered Newport Harbor on June 23, 1911, conveying William H. Taft to the Cotton Centennial in nearby Fall River.

Vincent Astor's ocean-going yacht, *Nourmahal,* brought President Franklin D. Roosevelt to Newport on Saturday, September 15, 1934, so that he could witness the first race of the 15th defense of the America's Cup between the American defender, *Rainbow,* and the British challenger, *Endeavour.* President Roosevelt returned in 1940 to make a comprehensive inspection and appraisal of the military and Naval installations of the Narragansett Bay area.

President Harry S. Truman, who was on his first vacation since attaining the nation's highest office, came to Newport in a driving rain on Monday, August 18, 1946. He made a brief inspection of the Naval Training Station and the Naval War College. After a lunch with College President Admiral Raymond A. Spruance, USN, and his wife, Truman returned to Quonset Naval Air Station where the official yacht, *Williamsburg,* was waiting to continue a vacation of cruising along the coast. Only a few years before, as a senator from Missouri, Truman had been in Newport to dedicate a servicemen's center.

President and Mrs. Dwight D. Eisenhower arrived at Quonset Naval Air Station on Wednesday, September 4, 1957, to begin the first of three month-long vacations in Newport, the others following in 1958 and 1960. One of the largest crowds to jam Washington Square was on hand to cheer the World War II leader, who consented to the civic reception held in front of the Old Colony House.

During their three vacations in Newport, the Eisenhowers often cruised around lower Narragansett Bay aboard the presidential yacht, *Barbara Anne.* Both did considerable sightseeing, and the president attended worship services in several of the city's churches. But most of all, Newporters will remember him as the first president in office to enjoy golfing at the Newport Country Club. Hardly a day passed that he was not on the course.

On Wednesday, September 4, 1957, President and Mrs. Dwight D. Eisenhower arrived in Newport to begin one of three month-long vacations they were to enjoy, through 1960, in the "City-by-the-Sea." After his formal reception at the Newport Naval Base, "Ike," conceding to the wishes of Newporters, attended a ceremony in his honor held outside the Old Colony House on Washington Square.

— *Newport Daily News*

John F. Kennedy was married to Jacqueline Bouvier in St. Mary's Church, on Spring Street, on September 12, 1953. The young United States senator from Massachusetts was frequently seen in Newport. As a young man he was also well known to other Rhode Island communities, often sailing in yacht club regattas.

Kennedy established the Summer White House at "Hammersmith Farm," on Ocean Drive. The mansion was the residence of Mr. and Mrs. Hugh D. Auchincloss, the stepfather and mother of Mrs. Kennedy. For three summers, 1961 through 1963, the Kennedy family enjoyed many forms of recreation — swimming, golfing, sailing, and entertaining numerous visitors to the

President and Mrs. John F. Kennedy attended masses in St. Mary's Church where they had been married in September 1953. Huge crowds gathered every Sunday outside the church to await his arrival and departure, and to cheer the young couple who made "Hammersmith Farm" the Summer White House. JFK knew Rhode Island well. He had sailed in regattas here, and took his PT-boat training at Melville, in Portsmouth. He was also a member of the board of directors of the weekly newspaper, *Narragansett Times*, published in Wakefield, an office he still held at the time of his unfortunate death.

— *Newport Daily News*

temporary White House. Huge crowds would gather outside St. Mary's Church on Sunday mornings to get a glimpse or to take pictures of the young couple as they emerged from the big front door and crossed the sidewalk to the waiting limousine. There were several Sundays like this, and it was a saddened Newport when President Kennedy was struck down by an assassin only a few weeks after he left the city — tanned and rested and ready to take on the burdens of the office he held.

Seventeen presidents in office came to Newport, as far as the records show, but almost all of the distinguished men who have attained the nation's highest elective office visited Newport at one time or another during their lives. These include James Buchanan, who was found to be just a "visitor" in Newport, and Franklin Pierce. Pierce came as a brigadier general of volunteers, and took a regiment of troops from Fort Adams to fight in the Mexican War. Within less than a decade, he became president. Richard M. Nixon made an official visit, as vice president, to Newport to confer with President Eisenhower. President Nixon had a previous association with Rhode Island; during World War II he was assigned to Quonset Naval Air Station.

In addition to the presidents and vice presidents already mentioned, the following came to Newport as vice presidents: Aaron Burr, John C. Calhoun, Schuyler Colfax and Garret A. Hobart. Few are the communities in the country that have such a distinguished roster of visitors. Newporters have always welcomed the nation's leaders with great enthusiasm, and once the visitors have settled in the community, their wish for privacy has generally been respected.

The Military

It was along the seacoast that Colonial America's settlements flourished into the first communities of importance. Newport, with the Atlantic Ocean as her southern boundary, was the most vulnerable to attack from the sea.

In April 1641, William Brenton, owner of the land that constitutes Brenton Point and the area around Fort Adams, set up a four-gun battery to protect his property. At about the same time,

the town provided a small armed boat to warn of any unwelcome strangers. Traine bands, consisting of a town's able-bodied men, were established — the beginning of the militia system. Regular drills were held on common land by these units which, with their crude weapons, composed the only defense against pirates or Indians.

King George II granted a charter to the Newport Artillery Company in 1741, and the unit has the distinction of being the nation's oldest active military organization. Its purpose was to train men to assume command, and was, like similar units in other Colonies, the prototype for contemporary reserve officer training programs.

In Rhode Island, many militia groups were organized. In 1667, the Island Troop of Horse was formed in Newport, the first military company in the Colony with a distinctive name. Some of the military companies flourished for many years, and others were

Detail of painting on stone, by J. P. Newell, of Newport in 1740. In the foreground is Fort George, on Goat Island. The original painting is in the possession of Trinity Church.

— *Redwood Library*

formed and disbanded according to the defense requirements of the state and nation. They bore such names as the Little Compton Artillery Company, Portsmouth Light Infantry, Jamestown Volunteers, Tiverton and Little Compton Dragoons, Newport Infantry, Tiverton Volunteers, Burnside National Guard (a battalion of Black citizens, one company of which was raised in Newport), Middletown Volunteers, Newport Troop of Horse, and the Aquidneck Rifles.

The British Admiralty early recognized the value of Newport's deep and natural harbor and quick access to the sea. Prior to the Revolutionary War, and during the British occupation of Newport, many of Great Britain's men-of-war were stationed in Narragansett Bay.

Persistence by Rhode Islanders finally convinced a stubborn Continental Congress to authorize a fleet to further engage the British forces. Appropriately, this first fleet was outfitted and provisioned in Newport.

Although Naval ships made frequent visits to Narragansett Bay, it was not until the Civil War that Newport's value for a growing Navy was given recognition. The United States Naval Academy was located here during that conflict. A part of Goat Island was utilized for training the midshipmen. In 1869, the first Naval torpedo station was established there. Committed to developing underwater ordnance, and a little later to the use of electricity, it became the most advanced school in the Navy, prior to the establishment of the Naval War College in 1884. The college was located on Coasters Harbor Island, where a year earlier the first Naval training station was founded. Both these installations, one to properly train seamen recruits and the other to provide courses of higher learning for commissioned officers, were brought into existence by the conviction and tenacity of Admiral Stephen B. Luce, USN.

Rhode Island is proud of its contribution to the defense of the nation. General Nathanael Greene was Washington's most-trusted general. Among others was Captain Stephen Olney, the first to breach the British defenses at Yorktown. The famous Naval heroes, Oliver Hazard and his brother Matthew Calbraith Perry, both commodores, distinguished themselves. The former was the hero of the Battle of Lake Erie; the latter, known for his expedition which succeeded in opening the ports of Japan to world trade, is further recognized as the "Father of the Steam Navy." When the *USS Monitor* was engaged in the world's first battle of ironclad ships, it was Newport's Lt. Samuel Howard who piloted the gun-carrying raft. Newport-born James L. Breese, Jr., was one of the crew of the Navy's flying boat, NC-4, the first airplane to fly over the Atlantic.

Several famous army officers did duty at Fort Adams. One was Indiana-born, Rhode Island-adopted Ambrose E. Burnside, who became commander of the Army of the Potomac. Another was General William S. Rosencrans. Braxton Bragg and John Magruder both served as generals in the Confederacy. Still later came General George W. Goethals, the builder of the Panama Canal, and General Lyman L. Lemnitzer, who was appointed in 1966 to head the United States European Command.

Major General James Parker, USA, who was born in Newark, N.J., in 1854, and died in New York, June 1934, served his nation beginning with duty in 1876 in what was called Indian Territory. He was with the units that pursued Geronimo, the famous Apache Indian chief, in 1886. General Parker served in the Spanish-American War and the Philippine Insurrection, and the Cuban Army of Pacification. He was awarded the Congressional Medal of Honor for distinguished gallantry at Vigan, Philippine Islands.

His active service continued into World War I with his mobilization of troops in Texas. He commanded the 32nd Division, and saw action near Armentiers and Chemin des Dames. He retired, after 42 years of duty, on February 20, 1918.

General Parker was married to Charlotte M. Condit in November 1879, and they observed their golden wedding anniversary at "Green Vale Farm" in Portsmouth. Mrs. Parker was related to the Barstow family, which owned the farm. Upon his retirement, it became their residence.

The general continued his interest in the Army, and when the Civilian Military Training Camps were established during the 1920s, he often visited Fort Adams and the summer training camp. The retired veteran is shown here reviewing the regiment, July 1930.

— *Newport Daily News Archives*

Old Fort Adams in the Civil War

J. A. Williams was one of the busiest and best of Newport's photographers during the middle decades of the last century. Maybe he "scooped" everyone with this rare photograph of General Robert Anderson, USA, who is standing second from the right, in the group around the cannon in the quadrangle of Fort Adams. Anderson was the commanding officer at Fort Sumter when it was fired on in 1861. Fort Adams was the general's last command. The picture was taken in September 1863.

— *Redwood Library*

Another picture by J. A. Williams, showing the drill field inside Fort Adams, September 1863. From the look of it, there was no lack of ordnance to protect the fort, Newport and Narragansett Bay. However, there were many times when the fort was without a sufficient garrison to muster a crew to man even one gun. Often, the Newport Artillery Company took over the post, until Federal troops arrived.

— *Redwood Library*

The Newport Artillery Company

△ The gun battery of the Newport Artillery Company, around 1885, at a drill in front of the then State House. Only four of the men are clean-shaven!

— *Newport Artillery Company*

▽ The Newport Artillery Company, marching in full strength, southward on Thames Street, past the Custom House, during the time of the Spanish-American War. Several pool players have halted their game and fill the balcony just below the sign reading "Storage."

— *Newport Historical Society*

△ Identified as members of the Newport Artillery Company, at the time of the Spanish-American War, the unit is at "The Basin," now Cardines Field, preparing to embark on waiting railroad coach cars. In the center of the activity, several ladies are arranging tables, preparatory to serving some good, home-style cooking to the departing militiamen.

— *Newport Daily News Archives*

▽ Photograph, of the Rogers High School Cadets' drum and bugle corps, taken during World War I. Note the caricature of the Kaiser on the bass drum.

— *Navy Y.M.C.A.*

Cover of sheet music for "Anchors Aweigh," dedicated to the class of 1907 midshipmen at the U.S. Naval Academy.

— U.S. Naval Academy Museum

The United States Naval Academy Band, in front of the Atlantic House. One band member was Charles A. Zimmermann, who lived on Green Street. Here was born his son, Charles, who became the Academy's musical director and wrote the music to "Anchors Aweigh."

— United States Navy

The Naval Academy at Newport

With the outbreak of the Civil War, the United States Naval Academy, in Annapolis, Maryland, was in danger. Maryland, a Border State, was sympathetic to the cause of the Confederacy. It was deemed advisable to remove the Academy, and Newport was chosen for its temporary location.

On May 8, 1861, the *USS Constitution* ("Old Ironsides"), followed by the steamer *Baltic*, arrived in Newport Harbor, trans-

porting the officers and professors and their families, and the midshipmen. At first, Fort Adams was selected for the use of the Academy, but the quarters were insufficient; within a few months, the Atlantic House, a fashionable hotel on Pelham Street, was requisitioned for the purpose. "Old Ironsides" was used to quarter some of the midshipmen, and was docked at Goat Island. The Academy remained in Newport through the summer of 1865, when it was re-established at Annapolis.

Newport's part in the continuity, growth and success of the Naval Academy was profound. Had there been no suitable location during the conflict, the Academy could very well have disintegrated, and many years would have been required to restore it to its rightful position in preparing young men to serve as Navy officers.

The arrival of "Old Ironsides" in Newport Harbor, with Captain George S. Blake, USN, superintendent of the United States Naval Academy, was greeted by Fort Adams with a 24-gun salute. Also shown in this picture is the steamer *Baltic*, with Fort Adams in the background. John P. Newell, one of Newport's famous artists of the last century, made this lithograph in 1861.

— *Redwood Library Collection*

Touro Park, which was just across Pelham Street from the Atlantic House, was used as a drill field for the "middies," who, during leisure time, used the park for football. Shown here are many of the young men who rose to high rank in the Navy, posed in front of the Old Stone Mill.

— Providence Public Library

Among the hundreds of midshipmen who were at Newport's Naval Academy were Robley D. Evans, Charles D. Sigsbee, French E. Chadwick, Charles S. Sperry, Royal B. Bradford, George A. Converse, Benjamin F. Tilley, Casper F. Goodrich, Colby M. Chester, Arent S. Crowninshield, Henry Glass, Chester V. Gridley, Theodore F. Jewell and Seaton Schroeder — just a few who attained their mark in the annals of the Navy.

Serving at various times on the faculty were several distinguished officers, among whom were Stephen B. Luce, Alfred T. Mahan, William T. Sampson and Edward Simpson.

During the period, several school ships were added to the Academy. One was the famous yacht, *America*. The *USS Marblehead* was also assigned to the Academy while it was in Newport. The *Marblehead* was the first steam-powered warship used to prepare the young midshipmen for the transition from wooden ships and sails to iron hulls and steam.

Although the United States Naval Academy remained in Newport for more than four years, its temporary location was, in a way, the beginning of the city's permanent association with the Navy. In 1869, Goat Island was designated as a torpedo-manufacturing facility. Its growth was phenomenal. Within a decade, it became the leading technical installation of the Navy, and top officers were assigned to the station. There, they not only learned about underwater ordnance but were taught much about chemistry and the new marvel, electricity. In 1883, the first Naval

Training Station was established on Coasters Harbor Island, and, a year later, Admiral Stephen B. Luce, USN, founded the Naval War College, the Navy's highest institution of learning.

Hundreds of civilians watch the apprentice seamen's review at the Naval Training Station. The review, held weekly, was open to the public. A row of battleships can be seen through the haze, outlined against the Jamestown shore. This photo was taken around the time of World War I.

— *Newport Historical Society*

Admiral William S. Sims, USN, was welcomed home to Newport on Friday, April 11, 1919. The commander-in-chief of the United States Naval Forces in Europe was the hero of the era, and Newport turned out the biggest military parade it has ever seen. A half-holiday was declared.

Admiral Sims arrived in Newport Harbor about mid-afternoon, aboard the destroyer *USS Sampson*, amidst the din of whistles from shipping craft and other boats in the harbor. A steam launch, carrying Mrs. Sims and a few other people, came alongside, and the admiral disembarked. He came ashore at the Government Landing and was given an escort of 60 flower girls.

He was officially welcomed by Gov. R. Livingston Beeckman and Mayor Jeremiah P. Mahoney. The officials, who included Congressman Clark Burdick, were assigned to carriages, and the big "Welcome Home" parade was underway. Admiral Sims passed through a huge floral arch at the head of the Government Landing, and the procession of 17 carriages headed south on Thames Street.

In this photograph, Admiral Sims has just passed the foot of Gidley Street. National, State and City officials, some wounded veterans, and members of the Grand Army of the Republic were in the other carriages.

Following the carriages was the largest turnout of military marchers ever seen in Newport. Accounts of the time report that 3,000 Army, Navy, Marines and Yeowomen were in the line of march. Another 3,000 Newporters, including band units, comprised the civic divisions of the parade. Naval company after company passed by in what seemed like an endless line of young sailors, who marched the three-mile route. They were reviewed by Admiral Sims from his residence, which was at the southwest corner of Kay Street and Mann Avenue.

Paying tribute to the admiral were delegations of clubs representing the Italians, Jews and Greeks of the community. There were units from the Sons of St. George; the Daughters of the American Revolution; the Women's Christian Temperance Union; the Odd Fellows; the Benevolent and Protective Order of the Elks; Weenat Shassit Tribe of Red Men; Loyal Order of Moose; Trinity Lodge of Elks; Salvation Army; Rogers High School Battalion; St. George's School Cadet Battalion; Camp Thomas of United Spanish War Veterans and the Camp Thomas Auxiliary; Knights of Columbus; Girl Scouts; Canton Newport Patriarch Militant; Y.M.C.A.; Y.W.C.A.; Army & Navy Y.M.C.A.; Daughters of St. George; Daughters of Isabella; Order of Vasa; Colonel Charles Young Association; Locals 121, 176, 534 and 1245 of the International Unions of America; Newport Police Department; Newport Fire Department; and the Ancient Order of Hibernians, among others.

— Newport Historical Society

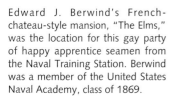

Edward J. Berwind's French-chateau-style mansion, "The Elms," was the location for this gay party of happy apprentice seamen from the Naval Training Station. Berwind was a member of the United States Naval Academy, class of 1869.

— Redwood Library

Above, On and Below the Sea

Captain Hugh L. Willoughby, in his flying machine, took this picture in September 1916, of the Naval Training Station. Barren Coddington Point dominates the center of the photograph.

— *Newport Historical Society*

Navy dirigibles made frequent visits to Newport. Often they would participate in fleet war games. In the first test of its kind, in August 1924, the giant airship *Shenandoah* successfully attached itself to the mooring mast on the *USS Patoka*, in Newport Harbor. In another successful experiment, in January 1928, the dirigible *Los Angeles* made a landing, off Newport, on the deck of the aircraft carrier *USS Saratoga*. Shown here is the *Los Angeles*, moored to the *Patoka*, in June 1930. The Jamestown shoreline can be seen in the background.

— *author's collection*

The *USS Salem* is seen here, being loaded with coal at the Bradford Coaling Station, later known as the Melville Coaling Station. Located on the west shore of Portsmouth, it was the Navy's first such facility.

Opened in 1904, it had a coal shed with a capacity of 10,000 tons and equipment that could unload in excess of 50 tons per hour from colliers. The largest war vessels could reach the wharf without any difficulty.

— author's collection

Torpedo boats at their slips at the Naval Torpedo Station. In the background are the overnight steamers to New York, the *Pilgrim* and the *Plymouth*.

— Newport Historical Society

In this photograph, taken during World War I, more than two dozen torpedo boats and destroyers occupy the piers of the Naval Torpedo Station.

— *Newport Historical Society*

The submarine, as an effective unit of the Navy, received many of its early tests in Newport waters. This 1898 photo shows the *Holland*, a small prototype of the bigger and more efficient undersea boats to come, hauled up on the ways of the Newport Ship Yard.

— *Newport Historical Society*

Captain Hugh L. Willoughby took this picture of the *Shark* in August 1905, at the Torpedo Station.

— *Newport Historical Society*

Leisure Time

It was Dr. Carl Bridenbaugh, of Brown University, who documented the fact that Newport was "America's First Resort." The distinguished author of numerous books on Colonial American history

The boardwalk at Newport Beach
(now known as Easton's Beach),
during the 1920s. This is where you
could find everybody on a Sunday.
It was different, then; it boasted a
roller coaster, shooting gallery,
penny arcade, and numerous con-
cessions selling popcorn and potato
chips. It had a convention hall and
a ballroom, where young couples
went to dance on cool summer
evenings. Among the many dance
bands that played here, Mal Hal-
lett's is still remembered.

— Providence Public Library

stated that, as early as the 1720s, families came to Newport from
the distant islands of the Caribbean and from the Carolina
Colonies to escape the heat and fevers of their regions.

Leisure-time activities, such as fishing, riding and hunting,
were indulged in by the settlers of the Colonies. For those who
could afford it, there was some traveling for pleasure. These trips,
however, were to nearby mountains or to springs. Eventually,
resorts were developed at places such as Saratoga and White
Sulphur Springs.

Newport had a big lead, which brought about her resort

status less than a century after the town was settled. It was accessible by sea, as well as land. The *Newport Mercury*, first published in 1758, and the oldest newspaper in America, has the distinction of running the first "society news" columns in this country. Not only did the editors list the arrivals of packet ships from Charleston and

other ports, they included the names of the passengers who made the voyage to Newport.

Newport Beach prior to World War I — crowds on the boardwalk, crowds on the beach, and a good crowd in the water. All eyes must have been drawn skyward when the airplane flew over the beach.

— Providence Public Library

In addition to a refreshing climate, Newport was where the action was. Horses were raced on the strand of Easton's Beach. There was music and dancing, pleasure boats and carriages for hire, backgammon and card games.

Newport was also a leading center for culture and the arts and crafts. These and other diversities were the attractions for hundreds of Southern and Caribbean families who were responsible for developing the seacoast community into a prestige resort a half-century before the Revolutionary War.

Soon after the War for Independence, many small hotels and numerous houses were open for the accommodation of the thousands that annually came to Newport. Later, hotel operators installed telegraph systems in their hotels so that bankers and brokers could keep in touch with their offices. George T. Downing and others saw the advantages of operating catering departments. They were complete in every way, from the preparation and presentation of food, to supplying silver, crockery, glass, lights and waiters. Yachting and picnicking groups were also accommodated, almost 150 years ago, by these enterprising men.

During the first part of the 1800s, Bostonians and affluent families from Philadelphia, Baltimore, Charleston and other distant places began to erect summer homes. After the Civil War, the impact of New York wealth was felt and the cottage colony

The maxi and the mini in bathing apparel of the early 1900s is shown off in this photograph taken in Jamestown.

— *Providence Public Library*

expanded. The cottages became bigger with each passing decade. The crest was reached during the period of 1880 to 1900, with the erection of such palace-sized cottages as "Belcourt," "Ochre Court," "Marble House," "Vinland," "Wakehurst" and "The Elms."

Newport was not only for the very wealthy. During the greatest part of the last century, and up to World War I, thousands of people came to Newport, for a day, during the summer, on excursion steamers. The steamers transported the hard-working

people who labored in the textile mills, factories and machine shops of Providence, Pawtucket, Fall River and New Bedford. Workers from New London, New Haven, Hartford and Bridgeport also came to the "City-by-the-Sea," on trips that lasted for two days. Train excursions poured additional hundreds into the busy resort from Boston, Taunton, Woonsocket and Worcester.

On weekdays, the excursion steamers kept busy carrying loads of women and children who looked forward to the annual church or Sunday school trip to the resort. Most of the excursionists headed for the public beach, but there were many who availed themselves of sightseeing. Those who could hired carriages to go around Ocean Drive, or out to "The Glen" at Portsmouth, or to Purgatory Rock in Middletown.

Warships in the harbor, band concerts at Fort Adams, clambakes at Bristol Ferry, and picnics at dozens of places appealed to Newport's visitors. In 1859, an item in the *Newport Daily News* gave a formula to follow for a successful picnic. It said, "The first requisite is a goodly array of pretty girls, then lemons, sugar, ice and tumblers, and if you are going where there are trees, ropes for swings, and perhaps a tent and boards for tables and seats — though many think it more romantic to use the ground for a seat and the lap of a pretty girl for a table."

Almost jammed like Times Square on a New Year's Eve was that part of Broadway at City Hall, one day in June 1918, when the famous "Garde Republicaine" band from France gave one of several concerts in Newport during a visit to the city (in this photograph, the band has been hemmed in, just to the right of the elm tree, by the crowd). Other concerts were presented at the Naval Training Station and Fort Adams. Automobile and trolley traffic was brought to a halt by the thousands who wanted to listen to the music of this superb band.

— *Navy YMCA*

Coaching

Coaching was one of the many diversions that members of the summer colony enjoyed during the Newport season. Coaching parades became annual events, and often vers were James Gordon Bennett, Jr., Fairman Rogers, Thomas Winans, Theodore A. Havemeyer and Alfred G. Vanderbilt.

Coaching drives went on the

several "whips" would get together and take moonlight drives around Ocean Drive. When the season ended, one of the top whips, Colonel William Jay, would coach back to New York. Other top dri- wane soon after the turn of the century. Four-in-hands were continued as horse show features, however, as shown in this photograph taken during the 1920s.

— *Newport Daily News Archives*

In 1968, a most successful event, ▷ the highlight of the season, was the meeting in Newport of the Carriage Association of America. Several four-in-hands took part in processions around Ocean Drive and along Bellevue Avenue.

At the Newport Casino (seen in upper photo), the parade of 14 horse-drawn carriages and coaches stopped to be photographed at that most appropriate of locations. A special event was held on the grounds of "Marble House," (lower photo) and a gymkhana was held at Freebody Park.

— *© John T. Hopf*

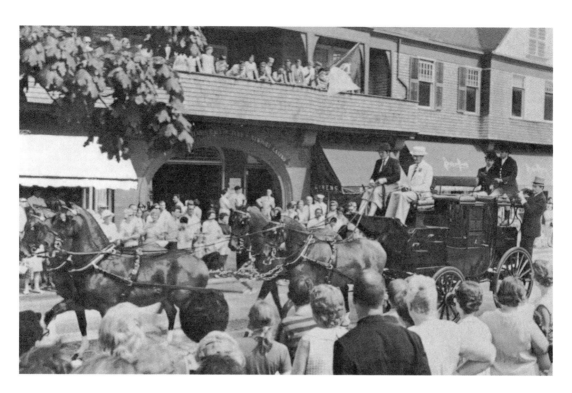

Golf

Newport produced two of this century's greatest golfers — W. Lawson Little, Jr., and John P. Burke (at right). Little, who was born at Fort Adams, won the British amateur golf championship two years in a row, in 1933 and 1934. He was the first American and the third golfer to accomplish this feat. He also took the U.S. amateur in 1934, turned pro in 1936, and won the U.S. Open championship in 1940.

But it was Johnny Burke that most Rhode Islanders watched. The likable redhead began his career as a caddy and, when he was 17, won the 1934 Rhode Island State Amateur Tournament. He made golfing history by winning the contest for the next two years.

In 1938, while a sophomore at Georgetown University, he took the national intercollegiate title. That year was also regarded as his best, and his contest in the Rhode Island Open against Jim Turnesa will stand forever in this state's golfing annals. Golf writers recall 1934, when he went to Brookline, Massachusetts, to compete against the nation's top amateurs. There he met another young golfer, W. E. Detweiler, and their match went to the 21st hole, with Detweiler ending the grueling contest by beating Johnny.

Johnny lost his life early in May 1943, in an accident in North Africa, where he was serving as a lieutenant in the Air Force. All Rhode Island grieved at the loss. In April 1946, when the Rhode Island Golf Association resumed its competitive program, it voted to establish the John P. Burke Memorial Fund Tournaments. The proceeds from this annual event are used to provide scholarships for worthy caddies. Frank Lanning, sports illustrator of the *Providence Evening Bulletin*, hailed the event as the "first major war memorial in the state."

— *Joseph H. Burke*

Any history of golf in America must include the part Newport played in the growth and development of the sport. In fact, a Newport summer resident, Theodore A. Havemeyer, is known as the "Father of Modern Golf in America." State and local golf courses have been played by such greats as Bobby Jones, Gene Sarazen, Francis Ouimet, Walter Hagen, George Von Elm, and Rhode Island's Glenna Collett Vare, the only woman to six times win the national women's amateur championship.

By 1893, golf was becoming an established sport in Newport. Not only was the Newport Golf Club (now the Newport Country Club) organized, but the fashion that went with the sport kept pace. Redfern's, known as a dress and habit maker ("By special appointment to H.R.H. the Princess of Wales, and H.I.H., the Empress of Russia"), featured the "Redfern Golfing Cape, as made for the Scotch and English clubs," which could be obtained at the Bellevue Avenue shop.

The Newport Country Club held the first amateur championship contest in September 1894, and because a similar contest took place at St. Andrew's, in Yonkers, New York, a conflict ensued. The result was the organization of the United States Golf Association, and the Newport club was among the half-dozen golf clubs to form the United States Golf Association (USGA). In September and October 1895, the first National Open Golf Championship was played on the Newport course. This was the same year that the present Whitney Warren-designed clubhouse was built.

In 1920, T. Suffern Tailer, one of Newport's summer colonists, began construction of his private nine-hole course, which he named Ocean Links. Almost three years were spent in building the course on Ocean Drive, and in 1924, 600 tons of a fine white sand were brought in freight cars, from Maryland, and carted to the course to replace the sand originally used to fill the traps.

For several years the highlight of Ocean Links was the annual Gold Mashie Tournament, originated in 1923, when Jesse P. Guilford and Jess Sweetser ended with a tie score of 291. In 1927, Sweetser, British and National champion, made a record of 287 on the course. T. Suffern Tailer, Jr., became one of Newport's outstanding amateur golfers and was always among the top players in many of the contests around the country.

These two photographs, of the Ocean Links course, date from the mid-1920s. At left, the master, Francis Ouimet, demonstrates his putting technique to young "Tommy" Tailer. Below, a large gallery follows players Edmund Driggs and Jess Guilford on the 7th hole of a Gold Mashie Tournament. Richard Van Nest Gambrill serves as referee.

— Patrick O'Neill Hayes

A view, from the Horseshoe Piazza, of the famous clock tower of the Newport Casino. The casino, built at the urging of James Gordon Bennett, Jr., was the first recreational facility of its type in America. The National Lawn Tennis Hall of Fame is located in a section of the famous building. The structure was designed in 1880-81 by the firm of McKim, Mead and White.

— *Preservation Society of Newport County*

Proper Bostonian, properly tennis-togged, Richard D. Sears was the first National Singles Champion, a title he won at the Newport Casino's first tennis tournament, in 1881. Sears continued for the next six years as the singles champion, retiring undefeated. *Lawn Tennis*, a treatise on the game, written in 1885 by Lt. S. C. F. Piele, was edited by Sears. In 1955, the singles champion was the first player to be invested in the National Lawn Tennis Hall of Fame.

— *International Tennis Hall of Fame*

In the photograph at right, William T. "Big Bill" Tilden accepts the Newport Casino's Invitation Tournament Singles Cup from James Stewart Cushman, 1930. Also shown is Francis T. Hunter, Tilden's doubles partner.

— *International Tennis Hall of Fame*

Tennis

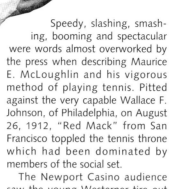

Speedy, slashing, smashing, booming and spectacular were words almost overworked by the press when describing Maurice E. McLoughlin and his vigorous method of playing tennis. Pitted against the very capable Wallace F. Johnson, of Philadelphia, on August 26, 1912, "Red Mack" from San Francisco toppled the tennis throne which had been dominated by members of the social set.

The Newport Casino audience saw the young Westerner tire out his opponent, a master of the "deadly chop stroke," and the crowning of a new singles champion. A *Providence Journal* reporter, describing the game, wrote, "Then the Californian stepped in to win. He took a position close to the net and was a veritable stone wall against the assault of Johnson, a besieging force, letting nothing get by him and killing with amazing effectiveness every return shot back by the runner-up."

McLoughlin, however, committed 84 errors to his opponent's 76; but it was the points that counted: 144 to 132. In 1913, he repeated the feat and kept the singles title.

— International Tennis Hall of Fame

Castle Hill has always been a favorite vantage point from which to see yachts go to the starting line off the Brenton light station. This picture, dated 1885, shows members of Newport's high society taking in the exciting scene of a New York Yacht Club race.

— *Providence Public Library*

The Newport Station of the New York Yacht Club was one of the busiest places along the waterfront, especially when the club's big yachts were in the harbor. In this photo, taken around the turn of the century, the view from Sayer's Wharf indicates the activity at other docks. Seagoing tugs and a coastal freighter are at adjoining piers and one of the big New York steamers is shown docked at Long Wharf.

— *Providence Public Library*

Yachting

Since the Colonial era, Newporters and summer visitors have enjoyed yachting and pleasure boating in Newport Harbor, Narragansett Bay and the Atlantic Ocean. Pleasure boats could be hired way back then, but it wasn't until the first half of the last century that big yachting became a part of the American leisure and sport picture. When the New York Yacht Club was organized in 1844, it made its first squadron cruise, that very season, to Newport. With the exception of only a few years, this cruise has always been included on the club's itinerary.

The city calls itself the "Yachting Capital of the World," a title it has carried with pride for a long time. In 1930, the America's Cup Races were first held off Newport, and in 1936, the biennial Bermuda Yacht Race was moved to this harbor.

Ever since the first defense of the America's Cup, in 1870, Newport has been host to all the yachts that have successfully kept the cup on this side of the ocean. Even though the earlier defenses were sailed off New York, the trial races were held in Rhode Island's waters.

The schooner yacht *America*, winner of the Queen's Cup in 1851 in a race, around the Isle of Wight, against the fleet of the Royal Yacht Squadron. The famous cup, named for this yacht, is the world's oldest international sporting trophy.

— *author's collection*

An 1895 advertisement, from the Providence *Journal*, promoting steamer excursions to the America's Cup yacht races in Newport.

— *author's collection*

Sir Thomas Lipton holds a model of Newport's famous Old Stone Mill. It was a gift from Newport's citizens, after he lost his fifth challenge for the America's Cup, in 1930.

Standing at far left is Mayor Mortimer A. Sullivan. It is believed that the presentation took place aboard Lipton's big steam yacht, *Erin*.

— *author's collection*

Weatherly, an unsuccessful defense contender in 1958, succeeded in defending the America's Cup against the Australian challenger, *Gretel*, in 1962. She was skippered by Captain Emil "Bus" Mosbacher. This picture was taken shortly after the 12-meter yacht had crossed the finish line.

— *author's collection*

Australia's first challenger, *Gretel*, is hauled out for her first checking at the Newport Ship Yard, soon after her arrival in 1962.

— *author's collection*

Captain "Bus" Mosbacher, who skippered the revolutionary 12-meter yacht, *Intrepid*, in 1967. He and his crew defeated the second challenger from Australia, the *Dame Pattie*.

— *author's collection*

Hotels

At first, boarding houses were used by visitors, and, by the early part of the 19th century, "cottages" were being built by wealthy Bostonians and others, to accommodate themselves and their guests. Newport had several hotels during the 19th century, but because of the large-scale building of private summer homes, it never became a "hotel town" in the same manner as fashionable Saratoga. Every one of the County's communities had summer hotels, and they were owned or managed by some of the best entrepreneurs in the business. So highly regarded by their patrons were the hotels, that music was written about them. An example is the "Stone Bridge Schottische," composed by F. Kielblock, and "Dedicated to the Patrons of the Hotel," in 1851.

A popular hotel was that owned by Seth Bateman, which he built on the Ocean Drive prior to the Civil War. In 1867, he built a water tower on the property; it was a replica of Newport's famous tourist attraction, the Old Stone Mill. The hotel was in use as an apartment house during the 1950s, and it subsequently was destroyed by fire. With the destruction in 1898, also by fire, of Newport's biggest hotel, the Ocean House, other smaller establishments catered to the city's visitors. During the 1920s, the need for larger and modern hostelries was evident in

Sheet music cover for "Stone Bridge Schottische," composed in 1851. It was dedicated to the patrons of the popular Tiverton hotel.

Fashionable Batemen's Hotel, seen here in a woodcut, was built before carriages could drive around the southern end of the island.

— *Rhode Island Historical Society*

71

many parts of Rhode Island. It was during this time that the Hotel Viking was built, and the 500-room Biltmore was erected in Providence. Both incorporated all the newest conveniences for guests, the Biltmore proclaiming that its 611 telephones, one in each room and others for use by the establishment, were twice as many telephones as could be found in the entire town of Tiverton!

The Ocean House, on Bellevue Avenue, photographed in 1890. It was destroyed by fire in 1898. The hotel was one of several fashionable establishments that catered to Newport's wealthy summer visitors, including President Ulysses S. Grant, circus magnate P. T. Barnum, and members of the diplomatic corps from several nations.

— *Preservation Society of Newport County*

The Bay View Hotel, in Jamestown, was built during the 1880s. Its tower, dominated by protruding dormer windows, made it nine stories high — perhaps the tallest hotel structure in the county.

Many distinguished and famous personalities have been guests in the area's hotels. In 1942, Tyrone Power, Dana Andrews, Jimmy Gleason and Anne Baxter stayed at the Bay View while they were in Newport making sequences for the classic World War II motion picture, "Crash Dive." Will Rogers chose to stay at the Hotel Viking, rather than use accommodations offered to him by the owner of a mansion.

— *Newport Historical Society*

Mansions

Leisure time in Newport, "Queen of Resorts," meant tennis, tea, concerts and horse shows at the Newport Casino; Ward McAllister-managed picnics at Southwick's Grove in Middletown; sport fishing, golfing, yachting, fox hunting, carriage drives, coaching parades, elaborate costume balls, afternoon tea dances, clam-

bakes, bathing and swimming, entertaining visiting presidents and royalty, attending band concerts and reviews at Fort Adams or the Naval Training Station; and watching the best polo teams in action. J. P. Morgan may have preferred to stay aboard his big, fast and luxurious yacht, *Corsair*, but many guests were lodged with their hosts and hostesses.

For this reason, the famous "summer cottages" were built. As each was built, it was intended to outdo others. Nowhere else in the world can such a concentration of "palaces" be found. Beginning with relatively modest 20-room structures in the 1840s, the peak was reached with the erection of magnificent European-style chateaux.

"Marble House" was completed in 1892 for William K. Vanderbilt. This view shows the east facade under construction.

— *Redwood Library Collection*

△ Pierre Lorillard built the first estate, named "The Breakers," in 1877-78. It was eventually sold to Cornelius Vanderbilt. Shown here is the great entrance hall of this house which was destroyed by fire in 1892. Vanderbilt built the present villa, of the same name, within the next two years.

— Redwood Library

▽ Charles Warren Lippitt, a descendent of a Rhode Island family that settled in Providence two years after Roger Williams established the Colony in 1636, was prominently identified with the cotton textile industry of the state. At the Republican Convention of 1896, his name was proposed for the office of vice president. He served as governor from 1895 through 1897. In 1899, he built "The Breakwater," more commonly known as "Lippitt's Castle," at the end of Ledge Road. It was demolished soon after his death in 1924, and on its site was erected "The Waves," the residence of famous architect John Russell Pope.

— Redwood Library

Around World War I, the cottages on Ochre Point were owned by William Woodward, T. Suffern Tailer, Louis B. McCagg, John R. Drexel and Mrs. Frederick Pearson.

— *Rhode Island Historical Society*

"Hammersmith Farm" was built in 1889 for John Auchincloss. On a Saturday night, January 12th of that year, Mr. Auchincloss gave a supper at the old Park House for 40 men who were engaged in the building of his summer cottage.

The property, which has remained in the Auchincloss family through the years, was the Summer White House during the time John F. Kennedy served as President of the United States. Mrs. Kennedy was the former Jacqueline Bouvier, and the stepdaughter of Hugh D. Auchincloss.

— *© John T. Hopf*

How We Got Around

It wasn't until 1716 that a Boston-to-Newport stagecoach line was established. Because of the geographical makeup of Newport County, much of the travel among its towns was by water. Conanicut Island, or Jamestown, had ferry service as early as the 1670s. Block Island, which until a few years ago was a part of Newport County, is 12 miles out in the ocean. Although there were many excursion steamers to the island, it wasn't until a steamer, *George W. Danielson,* went into commission on June 15, 1880, that regular service between Newport and Block Island was scheduled. Ferry service continues today to Prudence Island — part of the town of Portsmouth — but the run is made out of Bristol.

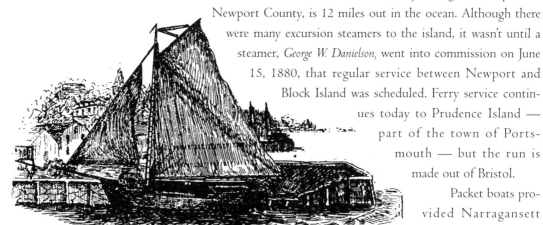

An 1846 illustration of a packet boat that provided ferry service between Newport and Jamestown.
— *Newport Historical Society*

Packet boats provided Narragansett Bay's first public transportation. In the 1800s, steamboats displaced the slower packet boats and opened up a whole new transportation system for Newport. Service was established to New York, and steamboats connected the ports of Narragansett Bay.

Newport was not served by a railroad until 1863. By that time, most communities of the East Coast had well-established rail lines. In contrast, however, Newport was one of the first cities to adopt the electric trolley. Local omnibus service eventually gave way to motorized buses, and long-distance bus lines eventually offered competition to the railroad.

For a century and a half, the only permanent link the communities of Aquidneck Island had with the mainland was the old Stone Bridge between Portsmouth and Tiverton. This was replaced in the 1950s with the multi-million-dollar Sakonnet River Bridge, an important segment in the high-speed highway that connects the Newport area with Boston. The old Stone Bridge was located just south of the new span and crossed the Sakonnet River at approximately the same place as the ferry it had replaced.

In October 1929, the opening of the Mount Hope Bridge, between Portsmouth and Bristol, replaced another ferry system.

Until that time, people from the Aquidneck Island towns had to take a trolley (later a bus) to Bristol Ferry, transfer, then transfer again to an electric transit line to complete the journey to Providence.

In August 1940, the Jamestown Bridge linked Conanicut Island with the mainland at Saunderstown, thus speeding travel between Newport and western points. In 1969, the $61 million Newport Bridge was opened to traffic. Spanning the East Passage of lower Narragansett Bay, it provided greater Newport County with direct automotive access to the west. The Newport Bridge replaced the oldest regularly scheduled passenger ferry service in the nation.

The three modern bridges have eliminated the inconveniences caused by old drawbridges and sometimes-sketchy ferry services. All of Newport County's principal sections are now con-

nected, and traffic can approach the island from three points of the compass, at all hours of the day.

The air age hit Newport with such an impact that the city boasts it had the first air service in the United States for the transportation of passengers. Newport's summer colony was responsible for bringing the service into existence, because its members, such as Vincent Astor and T. Suffern Tailer, found it most convenient to fly back and forth to New York in the matter of an hour or so. In June 1923, Grover Loening's air yachts were put into service between the two cities.

The steamer *Bay State*, the first of many commodious and elegant overnight steamers of the famed Fall River Line.

— author's collection

The aviation pioneers who resided in Newport's summer colony included Augustus T. Post, secretary of the Aero Club of America; Mrs. William K. Vanderbilt, Jr., who made her first flight over Garden City, New York, in 1910; J. Armstrong Biddle, the first aviator to reach 9,897 feet (in 1910); and Eleanora Sears, Boston sports enthusiast, whose first flight, in 1910, over Philadelphia, so aroused her enthusiasm for air travel that she declared she was going to buy an airplane and learn how to fly it. William Thaw, son of a wealthy summer colonist from Pittsburgh, flew planes from King Park in 1913. He later became one of the founders of the famed Lafayette Escadrille in France during World War I.

Just about all of aviation's immortals came to Rhode Island. Alberto Santos-Dumont was in Newport in 1902, hoping to find financial backers; Charles A. Lindbergh, Richard E. Byrd, Clarence Chamberlain, Jimmy Doolittle, Wiley Post and Roscoe Turner were among them.

Several locations on Aquidneck Island were utilized for airports during the 1920s and 1930s. After World War II, the Newport Air Park was developed. In 1960, it was taken over by the State and renamed Newport State Airport, one of the satellite facilities for Theodore Francis Green State Airport, in Warwick, which is a terminal for half-a-dozen major airlines.

Ferries

For almost three centuries, vessels of various descriptions, types and sizes have transported passengers, freight and domestic animals between Newport and Jamestown. It is believed that the sail ferry that started the Jamestown to Newport runs made its first trips

around 1670. In 1829, to shorten the travel time between the two islands, a short-lived experiment was made with a horse-powered ferry. Meanwhile, considerable thought was given to the cutting of a canal through the marshes of Jamestown in order to permit a ferry to go directly to the mainland at Narragansett or North Kingstown.

In 1873, a new, steam-powered ferry was put on the three-mile run across lower Narragansett Bay. A succession of newer and better ferryboats was acquired by the Jamestown Ferry interests to provide more efficient and faster service, in keeping with the public's demand for more expeditious connections with the mainland and points west.

The last two ferries to operate on the run, the *Newport* and the *Jamestown*, were the largest put into service. Each measured 194 feet in length, with beams of 49 feet. Each could transport 500 passengers and 58 automobiles. The historic ferry line, the oldest passenger ferry system in the nation, passed into oblivion with the opening of the Newport Bridge on June 28, 1969.

The Jamestown Ferry landing in Newport, around 1890. At the far left, the ferryboat *Conanicut* can be seen approaching the slip.

— *Rhode Island Historical Society*

A popular summer boat on the Jamestown-Newport ferry run, the *Conanicut* had a long career serving the transport needs of countless thousands, from 1887 until she was succeeded, in 1927, by the new *Governor Carr*.

— *Rhode Island Historical Society*

The ferryboat *Narragansett* was built in 1905 at Saunderstown. During World War I, she was acquired by the Navy, renamed *Toposa*, and put on the run between Newport and the Naval Torpedo Station on Goat Island. This photo was taken shortly before she was used for government work. In the foreground, a Navy launch, taxiing civilian visitors to a ship at its mooring, backs away from Government Landing.

— *Providence Public Library*

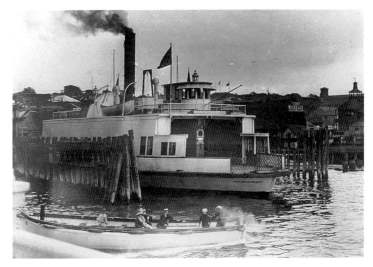

Another ferryboat, also named *Conanicut*, was one of many government-owned ferries that plied the inner harbor almost continuously, shuttling Naval personnel and civilians to and from the Naval Torpedo Station which once occupied Goat Island. The facility was phased out by the end of the 1950s, and ferry service was discontinued in the spring of 1960 when the island was declared "government surplus." From a humble beginning in 1869 with two employees, the station had grown to a World War II-era employment of about 15,000.

— *Rhode Island Historical Society*

Steamboats

For 90 years, 1847 to 1937, in fair and foul weather, the steamboats of the Boston, Newport and New York Steamboat Company, more popularly known as the "Fall River Line," daily made the 176-mile voyage from Fall River, via Newport, to New York. Beginning in 1847, with the steamer *Bay State*, the line's vessels maintained a reputation for being among the world's most elegant and commodious steamboats.

CONTINENTAL STEAMBOAT COMPANY.

DAILY EXCURSIONS!

Providence, Rocky Point, Conanicut Park, & Newport.

1878.   SUMMER ARRANGEMENT.   1878.

The Continental Steamboat Company's Steamers "CRYSTAL WAVE," "DAY STAR," "BAY QUEEN," and "CITY OF NEWPORT,"

Will run daily until further notice (Sundays excepted).   For hours of leaving, reference may be had to all of the daily papers.

Advertisement from the 1878 *Providence City Directory.*
— *author's collection*

In addition to the *Bay State*, the line included the *Empire State, Metropolis, State of Maine, Old Colony, Bristol, Providence, Newport, Pilgrim, Puritan, Plymouth, Providence* (second of this name), *Priscilla* and *Commonwealth*. The *Bay State* was 303 feet long, a large steamboat for her era; the *Commonwealth*, the last craft built for the line, was just over 455 feet long.

George Peirce, marine architect and superintendent of the line's repair shops in Newport, designed the *Pilgrim, Puritan, Plymouth, Priscilla* and the second *Providence*. They were all beauties, but *Priscilla* seemed to be a favorite. Roger Williams McAdam, author of several books about the Fall River Line, regarded the *Priscilla* as Peirce's masterpiece and wrote that she was the "acknowledged queen of the great ships of the Fall River Line." W. King Covell of Newport, an authority on the line, once noted that "The *Priscilla* was, to her age (1893), what the clipper ship *Flying Cloud* was 50 years earlier." *Priscilla*, along with the second *Providence*, *Plymouth*, and *Commonwealth*, was in service until 1937, when a strike, coupled with operating deficits, brought an abrupt end to the oldest passenger-line service of that time.

Because the steamers of the line were the best products of marine architects and master shipbuilders, many innovations were introduced aboard them. The second *Providence*, for example, had a telephone in every stateroom. The *Pilgrim* was one of the first ves-

Steamer *Block Island*, whose career was identified with Norwich, New London and Watch Hill, is shown here at her New London landing in 1882. She made test runs out of Newport during July of that year. She was a day boat and was 199 feet long and "substantially built." By 1915, she was back in Newport and used by the New England Steamship Company as a boarding home and diner for the company's laborers and deckhands. In 1930, she was towed to Dyer Island, off Melville, and burned.

— *author's collection*

sels in the world to be completely illuminated with electric lights, and the steamer *Commonwealth* was one of the earliest American coastal ships to install a wireless system.

The ships of the Fall River Line carried princes and presidents. Of the latter, Presidents Fillmore, Polk, Grant, Cleveland, Harrison and both Roosevelts were recorded as passengers on the big white floating palaces. Reminders of the line are the two big anchors in Vanderbilt Park, on Broadway, which were used by the huge overnight liners.

Steamer *George W. Danielson* provided the first regularly scheduled service from Providence to Block Island, via Newport.

— *author's collection*

Also called the "Queen of Narragansett Bay," the steamer *Mount Hope* proudly bore the moniker for almost half a century. Designed by the famous marine architect George Peirce, of Newport, she could carry over 1,000 passengers on her run from Providence to Newport and Block Island.

In 1897, she made the run from Newport Harbor to Old Harbor (Block Island) in an hour and a half! Built in 1888, her long career ended in 1935 when she came to rest with other hulks in that section of the Providence River that was known as "Rotten Row." In 1961, an old salt who had served on her and other Bay vessels said, "The *Mount Hope* is still the best damned boat that ever came up the bay."

— *author's collection*

Called the "Queen of Narragansett Bay," for almost a quarter of a century (1870-92) the steamer *Eolus* plied the waters between Newport and Wickford, carrying passengers and freight. She was the connecting link with the fast New York trains which stopped at Wickford, and many visitors preferred the trip on the *Eolus* to continuing by train to Providence and transferring to a "down river" steamer. On her trips made Wednesday, August 25, 1871, over 900 passengers came over to Newport on the *Eolus*.

This steamboat was extensively used by Newport's "400." Furniture and furnishings from their New York apartments, as well as horses and carriages, were shipped by train to Wickford, then ferried to Newport. Often, the *Eolus* would make special trips. James R. Keene chartered her at least three times during the winter of 1881-82, just to convey him from Wickford to Newport! A frequent user of the *Eolus* was Chester A. Arthur, who vacationed in Newport while he was vice president and president of the nation.

Newporters admired the gilded reliefs, of the Old Stone Mill, which were the principal ornaments on each of the paddle wheel housings. The *Eolus* was laid up after the season of 1892 and sold the next year.

— *Rhode Island Historical Society*

The tug *Aquidneck*, built in Boston in 1889 for Gardiner B. Reynolds, was chiefly a working vessel but was also much in demand by local groups for excursions around lower Narragansett Bay. Ten years after her Newport debut, she was taken to New London where she went into the service of the Thames Tow Boat Company.

— *Redwood Library*

The steamers *Awashonks*, *Queen City* and *Islander* were the boats that sailed out of Providence and down the Sakonnet River to Sakonnet Point. This photograph of the *Islander* is from a 1908 post-card. The steamboats serving the growing summer colony in that section of Newport County replaced a sailing packet line in 1885.

— *author's collection*

During the 19th century, Prudence Island, in the middle of Narragansett Bay, developed as a summer resort. Cottage colonies were built by families from Bristol, Providence and other communities on the upper part of the bay. Although the island is a part of the town of Portsmouth, regular transportation to Prudence Island is via Bristol.

The steamer *Prudence*, shown here at her Sandy Point dock, served the island for about 40 years. This photograph is from a 1922 postcard. The message on it, addressed to an East Providence resident, reads, "We are enjoying ourselves immensely...expect to return Saturday or Sunday...whichever day the tide is right to bring the flivver back. Lovingly, Florence."

— *Chester E. Gilroy*

The steamer *Bristol* (sister ship of the *Providence)* plied the waters between New York and Bristol.

— *author's collection*

The *Commonwealth,* part of the Fall River Line, provided the traveling public with luxurious appointments that surpassed those found aboard trans-Atlantic ships. For the passengers' enjoyment there was the two-deck Venetian-Gothic Grand Saloon, the Empire Saloon of mahogany and gold, the English Renaissance Café, and the Adams Saloon, distinguished by its green paneling. Gourmet meals were served in the Louis XVI dining room on the fourth deck.

— *Providence Public Library*

The *Priscilla* made history, early in October 1923, when radio programs were picked up from shore stations and re-broadcast throughout the ship.

— *author's collection*

The *Chauncey M. Depew* was one of the last of the big steamers to make the run from Newport to Block Island. She is shown here at her Newport landing on Sunday, September 5, 1948, code flags flying in keeping with the Labor Day holiday weekend.

— *author's collection*

By Land and Air

The Broadway Stage Co. was operated for a few years during the 1880s and 1890s by Michael E. Fitzgerald. Such a large vehicle would have to be drawn by at least two horses; a close look reveals the legs of a second animal.

— *Providence Public Library*

Many Newporters can recall when the corner of Bath Road (now Memorial Boulevard) and Bellevue Avenue looked like this. The trolley route to Newport Beach originated at the car barn on Commercial Wharf and was the first segment of a system that eventually provided transportation to various parts of the city and the Naval Station. The first run was made on August 3, 1889. The average time to make the trip from the car barn to the beach was 12 minutes. This photo was taken in 1906.

— *Providence Public Library*

AUTOMOBILE RACES

TO BE HELD AT
AQUIDNECK PARK,
NEWPORT, R. I.,
FRIDAY, AUGUST 30, AT 2 P. M.
ADMISSION ············· 50 CENTS.

Advertisement, from the August 30, 1901, *Providence Journal.*

— *author's collection*

The desire of automobile manufacturers to replace horses with motorized horsepower, and the early acceptance of vehicles by Newport's "400," contributed to the growth of this nation's automotive industry. America's first auto race was the feature of the State Fair, in Cranston, on September 7, 1896, when Riker Electrics defeated the gasoline-powered entries of the Duryea Motor Wagon Company.

On September 7, 1899, no less than 19 electrically-driven carriages, bedecked in flowers, comprised the first auto parade in the country. The colorful event took place on the big lawn at O. H. P. Belmont's chateaustyle estate, "Belcourt." In 1900, the first auto races in this area were staged in Middletown, with some of the cars attaining speeds of almost 20 miles per hour.

Aquidneck Park, in Middletown, was the site for the 1901 races. The owner-drivers' names were from the Social Register: Mrs. Joseph Widener, Mrs. O. H. P. Belmont, Foxhall Keene, Hugh L. Willoughby, Reginald Vanderbilt, O. H. P. Belmont, Henry Howard, Baron de Morogues, James L. Breese and William K. Vanderbilt, Jr., among others. Vanderbilt, with his "Red Demon," made the fastest speed, attaining a mile in one minute, 28 seconds! He was regarded as the "Father of Automobiling in America."

In this photograph, taken at the August 30, 1901, races, Willoughby is at the controls of "22." Paulding Fosdick's entry, "31," featured a smokestack for emission of exhaust. The driver of car "34" cannot be identified. The race was the first in the United States to be held on a circular course.

— *Newport Historical Society*

The Pierce Arrow

"*Marble House*" *Newport*

Licensed Under Selden Patent.

The next unsold delivery dates of 1911 Pierce-Arrow Cars are November and December—on orders placed at once.

FOSS-HUGHES MOTOR CAR CO.
Exclusive Dealers in Pierce-Arrow Cars

18 SNOW STREET.

Fashionable Newport has always appeared as background for national advertisements. Years ago, a cigarette company showed the clock tower of the Newport Casino.

Illustrated here is Marble House, which made an appropriate setting for the 1911 Pierce-Arrow. This ad appeared in a September 1910 issue of the Providence *Journal*.

— *Preservation Society of Newport County*

On August 12, 1912, Jack McGee, a young Central Falls flyer, made his first solo flight. About two weeks later he was an attraction at Newport Beach, giving demonstrations with his "flying machine," and taking daring passengers up for 10-minute flights. He also "cracked up" when an air pocket caused him to lose control of his aircraft; he managed a forced landing on a field near St. George's School, but the landing gear hit a blind ditch. A wing was damaged in what has been documented as the first airplane accident in the state.

In this pair of *Newport Daily News* photos, McGee is shown at the controls of his aircraft and flying over the bench area. As can be seen in the lower photo, practically all of Easton Point at that time was open farmland.

— *Newport Historical Society*

Hugh deL. Willoughby, pioneer automobilist and aeronaut, made his first airplane flight, in 1909, over Atlantic City in a plane of his own construction. He obtained a patent that year for double rudders with inverse and simultaneous action — an invention put to great use by Wright, Curtiss and other aviation pioneers.

Willoughby brought his hydro-aeroplane, *Pelican II*, to Newport in 1912 for a series of tests that proved to be unsuccessful. He operated from a "camp" he established at King Park, conveniently near his summer home, "The Chalet."

The aviation enthusiast was the first to fly from Newport, and fortunately much of his work was documented by photography. Above, his "Model F" — a most fragile-looking craft — is shown being assembled at King Park for flights made in 1915.

Below, a more substantial plane was photographed with Willoughby and unidentified others on the day of his "long flight," August 21, 1916. The Curtiss flying boat flew over the city and harbor at a speed of 60 miles per hour. Willoughby took photographs of the area from an elevation of 200 feet, and then took the controls from his co-pilot and climbed to 2,000 feet.

In 1894, Willoughby was instrumental in organizing the Naval Reserve in Rhode Island. He died in 1939 at the age of 84.

— *Newport Historical Society*

The Colony House, or Old State House, at the head of Washington Square. Construction was begun on the structure in 1739 and it has the distinction of being the second-oldest United States capitol building.

Much history has been made within its walls. From the middle of the last century, this building and the Old State House in Providence served as capitols of this small state. Until 1900, when all the activities of the General Assembly were transferred to the new capitol building in Providence, every governor of Rhode Island was inaugurated at ceremonies held on its balcony.

It served as the first armory and headquarters of the Newport Artillery Company. In 1756, in one of its rooms, Dr. William Hunter delivered the first lectures in America on medicine and anatomy. From its balcony, the Declaration of Independence was read as soon as the news of this event reached Newport. During the Revolution, the British and French used the building as a hospital, and in it chaplains of the French Expeditionary Forces said the first Catholic masses in Rhode Island.

In March 1781, General Washington came to Newport to confer with Count de Rochambeau, of France. The two leaders met in the Senate Chamber and mapped the plans which led to the British surrender at Yorktown. Here Washington was made a Marshal of France, in accordance with the wishes of King Louis XVI that there could only be one leader of an allied army.

Countless dignitaries have been received at public receptions in Newport's Old State House, including Washington, Lafayette, Jefferson, Grant, Hayes and Eisenhower.

The building served as a community house for many years. Lectures of all kinds have been given here, and exhibits of paintings have been held.

George Rome, who had an extensive brewery which stood near the First Baptist Meeting House, utilized the cellar of the building. According to a 1770 account, the beer he made was conveyed in an aqueduct to the cellar, where it was fermented and sold.

The universal symbol of hospitality, the pineapple, is part of the ornate motif of the balcony's pediment. Newport has long used this symbol, and many pineapple motifs can be seen over the doorways of buildings in the city. It is believed that the Old State House pineapple was carved by James Moody, a Newport cabinet maker, at about the time the building was erected.

— *Preservation Society of Newport County*

In the Public Service

The concern for the health, happiness and welfare of the people of Rhode Island dates back to 1647 when the General Assembly ordered "that each Towne shall provide carefully for the reliefe of the poore, to maintayne the impotent, and to employ the able, and shall appoint an overseer for the same purpose."

In 1654, the General Assembly received complaints that no days had been set aside for "Men servants, maid servants and children to recreate themselves." The incivility towards these people was considered and the Colony government ordered each Town to select days for rest and recreation.

By their efforts to assist those of less fortunate circumstances, many social and fraternal groups have, through the years, strengthened the laws. One of the earliest such organizations in Newport was the Fellowship Club, which was founded in 1752 by 19 seafaring men who lived in constant danger when engaged in their work upon the high seas. The Fellowship Club changed its name to the Newport Marine Society, in 1785, when its Colonial charter was altered in conformity with the creation of state government.

Part of its charter, preserved in the Newport Historical Society, tells of the purposes of the organization. It was formed to give "relief [to] unfortunate mariners as well as great assistance to the widows and helpless orphans of the deceased members. . . [and it was] desirous of establishing Funds for the relief of the unfortunate and destitute and for the promoting of the useful marine knowledge." This worthy society existed until 1900.

Throughout all our communities there is evidence that our people do much to

The Newport Asylum (shown below in an 1834 engraving) was built on Coasters Harbour Island in 1820 for the care and support of the poor. In 1880, Newport's citizens voted 882 to 161 to cede the island to the State of Rhode Island.

On March 12, 1881, the General Assembly gave approval to cede the island to the Federal government for the purpose of establishing the nation's first shore-based Naval training station. The 92-acre parcel was valued at $192,000. On June 4, 1883, the Federal government declared, "...the Naval station at that place has been permanently established." In 1884, in the stone structure, Rear Admiral Stephen B. Luce, USN, established the world's first naval war college.

Ground was broken on September 14, 1891, for a new college building. The architect was George C. Mason, of Newport. The old building became the Administration Building. In 1964, it was designated a National Historic Landmark, and in 1978 was converted to the Naval War College Museum (seen in the photograph at left).

— *Naval War College Museum*

The old Custom House, at the corner of Thames and Franklin Streets, was built in 1829. The site is now occupied by the Federal Building, which houses the city's main post office and custom house.

— *Newport Historical Society*

assist the needy and to develop programs for our young that will make them worthy citizens. Church organizations and service clubs, through their members, have donated much in the way of time, money and personal resources. Individuals have provided such needed facilities as the Seamen's Church Institute and the Navy YMCA. Ethnic groups, in addition to supporting local causes for community betterment, have their own beneficent societies.

Newport is indeed fortunate that its citizens of past years organized worthy cultural institutions such as the Redwood Library, Newport Historical Society and the Art Association of Newport. It is proud of its new, million-dollar public library. These resources have enriched us all.

The United Fund is an outstanding example of the harmonious relations enjoyed by the area communities and the Naval installations. A significant part of each year's drive for funds comes from the officers, enlisted men, and families of the forces ashore, as well as the forces afloat.

The Boy Scouts, Girl Scouts, and similar groups of organized young people, have a proud history of contributing to their respective communities. And, typical of how things are done in Newport, it was through the efforts of a Navy admiral that the first troop of Boy Scouts was formed.

The Newport Hospital, founded in 1873, filled the need for the community to comfort and cure the injured and sick. It came into existence as the result of a serious injury experienced by one of Newport's black citizens. There was no hospital to minister to the suffering man; The *Newport Daily News* made a campaign out of the incident, and civic response was immediate.

Charlotte Cushman, America's first internationally recognized actress, who built a summer cottage/retirement home in Newport, was one of the first to raise money for the hospital. On the evening of August 20, 1872, she gave a dramatic reading in a local theatre. In 1874, Henry Ledyard donated two lots on Howard Avenue (now Powel Avenue) which gave "the hospital really a frontage on Howard Avenue, and will greatly add to the pleasantness of the location."

The churches of the city became one of the principal sources of income for the growing facility. "Hospital Sundays" were held from time to time, and collections made among the congregations for the hospital's benefit. Typical of such a Sunday was August 8, 1875, when over $2,500 was collected by the churches. Trinity Church came through with $866, followed by the United Congregational Church with $825.07. Others contributed as follows: All Saints Chapel, $229.26; Catholic Church, $200; Unitarian Church, $111.20; Emmanuel Church, $92.30; Central Baptist Church, $65; First Methodist Episcopal, $50; Second Baptist Church, $43; and Zion Church, $27.75.

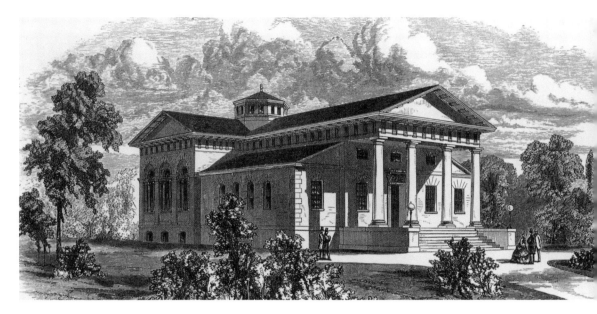

Newport's first cultural institution was the Redwood Library and Athanaeum. It was an outgrowth of the Philosophical Society of Newport (1729). The company was incorporated in 1747, and the Peter Harrison-designed edifice was constructed in 1748. This print shows the addition of 1858. Subsequent additions were made in 1879, 1913 and 1940.

British officers used the library as a club during the Revolutionary War, and the building was also utilized by the General Assembly for some of its meetings. Throughout the years, the library has sponsored countless exhibits and hosted series of lectures and educational pro-

grams. In May 1917, the directors voted to provide a reading and writing room for enlisted men of the armed services.

Back in 1762, its librarian exercised much patience when he published a notice in the *Newport Mercury,* on July 30, concerning missing books and stating, "Whoever have any of the above-said books, are desir'd to return them into the Library aforesaid, within a Month from this Date."

Redwood Library, the nation's oldest continuously used library building, was designated a National Historic Landmark in 1962.

— *Rhode Island Historical Society*

"Deprived as we heretofore have been of the invaluable rights of free citizens, we now (with a deep sense of gratitude to the Almighty Dispenser of Events) behold a Government erected by the majesty of the people, a Government which gives to bigotry no sanction, to persecution no assistance; but generously affording to all liberty of conscience and immunities of citizenship, deeming everyone, of whatever nation, tongue, or language, equal parts of the great Governmental machine." So wrote Moses Seixas, Warden of the Hebrew Congregation of Newport to President George Washington, August 17, 1790, as part of a congratulatory message to him on his election as president of the United States.

In his reply of August 21, Washington utilized a portion of Seixas' profound and beautiful words when he wrote, "For happily the Government of the United States, which gives to bigotry no sanction, to persecution no assistance, requires only that they who live under its protection should demean themselves as good citizens, in giving it on all occasions their effectual support."

Touro Synagogue, which stands as a shrine of true religious freedom, was built in 1762 and dedicated the following year. It is the oldest Jewish house of worship in America.

Its exterior has retained its simple and dignified appearance through the years. On August 31, 1947, Touro Synagogue was designated a National Historic Site. This woodcut originally appeared in *Harper's New Monthly Magazine*, August 1874.

— *Newport Historical Society*

"Lord, Thou hast been our dwelling place in all generations." So read Rev. George W. Quick, D.D., of the Second Baptist Church, quoting from the Scriptures, at the impressive cornerstone-laying ceremony of the Army & Navy Young Men's Christian Association, on the morning of November 9, 1910 (see Navy YMCA photograph, above). Today, the five-story structure is known as the Navy Y, but through the years it has been home and hotel for millions of servicemen of all branches.

Regarded as one of the most magnificent gifts to the city, the land and building were presented to the YMCA by Mrs. Thomas J. Emery, of Cincinnati, who was a summer resident at "Mariemont," in Middletown.

Rhode Island's United States Senator, George Peabody Wetmore, delivered the principal address at the ceremony, which was attended by Rear Admiral Raymond P. Rodgers, USN, president of the Naval War College; Rear Admiral Stephen B. Luce, USN (ret.); and Rear Admiral French E.

Chadwick, USN (ret.). Admiral Rodgers was a nephew of the Rhode Island-born Naval hero brothers, Commodores Oliver Hazard Perry and Matthew Calbraith Perry.

The Army was represented by detachments of Coast Artillery and the Post Band from Fort Adams. Marines, seamen gunners from the Naval Torpedo Station classes, and four companies of Naval apprentices from the Training Station represented the Navy. Lt. Frank T. Evans, USN, was in charge of the Naval detachments. Evans later became the commanding officer of the Naval Training Station.

The Newport Young Men's Christian Association was incorporated in 1888. Its first meeting rooms were in the brick building that still stands on the southwest corner of Touro and Thames Streets.

The Y next moved to Mary Street and occupied the David Cheseborough house (seen in the Preservation Society of Newport County photograph, at right). It was a handsome edifice, built in

1737 and subsequently demolished, in 1908, to make way for the large brick building that was to replace it. The new structure was made possible by a $100,000 gift from Alfred G. Vanderbilt, in memory of his father, Cornelius Vanderbilt.

Old Trinity's spire has dominated Newport's skyline since 1726. This heretofore unpublished etching, by famed Newport calligrapher and stonecutter, John Howard Benson, delineates the beauty of the towering and graceful steeple.

The building's elegant workmanship is a monument to Newport's artisans, who were very productive during the town's "Golden Age." It has long been considered Colonial America's most beautiful church.

— *Trinity Church*

The interior of Trinity Church, ▷ showing the three-tiered "wine glass" pulpit, the only one of its kind in the United States.

— *Preservation Society of Newport County*

△ At the left of the photograph is Newport Hospital's original building; the addition, on the right, was built in 1893.

— *Newport Hospital*

▽ Newport Hospital's Hazard Administration Building, seen here in a circa 1930s photograph. The structure was erected in 1900, using funds from the estate of John Alfred Hazard.

— *Newport Hospital*

Back in Colonial days, the cry of "Fire!" was cause for great concern. Equipment was crude and it was very difficult for volunteers to save a flaming building. As early as 1641, the Colony prohibited fires from being kindled "by any whatsoever to runn at randome, eyther in Medows or Woods; but what by him that so kindled it shall forthwith be put out, that it damnifie none. And that if damage shall accres, satisfaction to the utmost shall be awarded."

Torrent Engine Company, No. 1, was organized in 1725, according to one account, and received its first piece of equipment in 1736. Other volunteer units in Newport bore such names an Rough and Ready; Hercules Fire Engine Company; Protection Engine Company, No. 5; and Aquidneck Engine Company, No. 3.

The Deluge Engine Company, No. 6, was disbanded in 1867. An account of the time noted that its machine "is a crazy old tub and has been entirely useless for two or three years." Although volunteer companies did render great service for many years, the City of Newport organized a professional fire department in 1885.

In the Newport Fire Department photo, at top, is the hose cart of

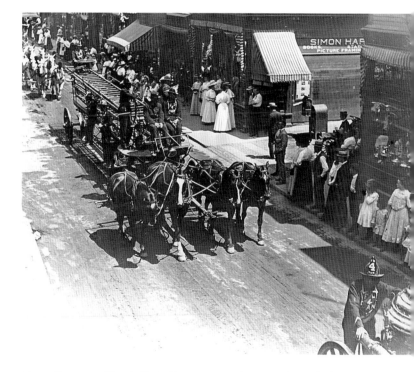

Hope Company, No. 4. Note the dog, seated by the driver. A century ago, this unit was stationed on Oak Street. With the formation of a regular fire department, the organization's historic name was changed to Hose Company, No. 4.

Turn-of-century photo of a fireman's parade, above, originally was published in the Newport *Daily News*.

— *Newport Historical Society*

On Memorial Day in 1922, several troops of Girl Scouts, including one of black citizens (third troop in the line), paraded in honor of those who gave their lives in the service of the nation. The troops are shown heading north on Thames Street, at the intersection formed by Washington Square and Long Wharf.

— *Newport Daily News*

Laws were made so that man could conduct his personal and business life in an orderly manner. Those who broke the laws were penalized. One of the first orders of business for a newly founded community was the establishment of a code by which its inhabitants could live within the law.

But laws are made to be broken, so the saying goes, and our early settlers were cognizant of man's weaknesses. Portsmouth was settled less than a month when at its general meeting of March 23, 1638, it was ordered that a "Howse for a prison...shall forthwith be built."

Early records indicate that a Colony prison was erected in Newport in 1658, in the vicinity of the city's present police station; subsequent prisons were built in 1680 and 1772.

The first police station in Newport was built in 1867 in the middle of Market Square and was used until 1914 when another was built on the north side of the Square. This was in use until 1965, when the Department moved into the 1772 former Newport County Jail. In 1985, the Department moved into its new, high-tech headquarters on Broadway.

◁ The photo at left probably was taken soon after the 1914 structure was occupied. The sergeant is literally surrounded by paperwork. In 1958, the department replaced the old system of "booking," in use since 1900, with a modern record-keeping system.

— *Newport Police Department*

Although the photograph is undoubtedly posed, policewomen were a reality at Newport Beach.

— *Newport Historical Society*

From 1969 to the Present

When the foregoing pages of this book were first published in 1969, on the occasion of Bank of Newport's 150th anniversary, the Newport Bridge (since renamed the Claiborne Pell Bridge) was

Opening day of the Newport Bridge, June 28, 1969. The last two ferries that provided service between Newport and Jamestown can be seen at the middle of the photograph. The construction of the bridge eliminated the three-centuries-long need for such transportation between the islands.

— © John T. Hopf

nearing completion. With a price tag of almost $19 million dollars, the bridge was opened to traffic on June 28th of that year. It was hailed as the world's second-longest suspension span, and at the dedication ceremonies U.S. Senator Claiborne Pell stated that it would open a new gateway to southern Rhode Island, as well as provide commercial and recreational opportunities for the entire state.

The first edition of *Portrait of Newport* ended with the following statement: "In the spirit of recalling all the good that has been bestowed upon us, we join with the people of our area in looking forward to a future that will be as promising and as generous as the eras recalled within the covers of this book." With this 1994 edition, we add what has transpired during the past 25 years, in celebration of the Bank of Newport's 175th anniversary.

The past 25 years have been nothing short of amazing; just witness the waterfront redevelopment that has taken place in our city's center and on Goat Island. We've also seen a steady increase in year-round tourism. Programs such as the month-long Christmas in Newport liven December, while attracting hundreds via motor-coach tours. Other festivals are held from January through March. Cruise ships such as the *Queen Elizabeth 2* have come as early as April and returned during the period once referred to as the "Late Season" by Newport's society set.

All this has taken place despite the diminishing Navy fleet presence in Newport. In 1973, it was announced the fleet would be taken away. The ensuing years brought the return of a few ships, additions to the Naval War College, and the assignment of new schools to the base. In 1994, the last of a dozen ships left — marking the first time in more than 150 years that not a single ship was assigned to Newport. Recently, horizons have brightened with news of a Naval Underseas Weapons Center expansion that would more than make up for the loss.

While *Portrait of Newport* dealt with history, *Portrait of Newport II* is more of a review. We hope you enjoy this unique presentation. It covers a multitude of events and changes — including many you've witnessed yourself — that are destined to become part of our city's glorious history.

Cultural Offerings

By now, Newport's summer music festivals have become legendary. Organized in 1968, the prestigious Newport Music Festival presents classical artists from all over the world. This annual event, a series of virtuoso performances staged in the fabled mansions, lasts for several weeks. In 1979, the Warsaw Chamber Opera, sponsored by the Newport Opera Festival, won special acclaim from a Beechwood mansion audience.

The period from 1969 to 1994 also saw the demise and

Ashore and afloat, big crowds turn out for the annual Newport Jazz Festival. This was the scene at the 1993 Festival, held at Fort Adams State Park.

— © 1993, John T. Hopf

rebirth of the Newport Jazz Festival and the Newport Folk Festival. A resurgence in popularity for these genres of music has led to successful runs for both in recent years.

It was reported that 80,000 attended the first Newport Jazz/Rock Festival, July 4 to 6, 1969. July 10, 1970, has also been recorded as a unique day in the history of the Newport Jazz Festival. It opened with a tribute to Louis "Satchmo" Armstrong, as a celebration marking his 70th birthday. Among the participants for the gala were gospel singer Mahalia Jackson, Dizzy Gillespie, Providence native Bobby Hackett, The Eureka Brass Band, the Preservation Hall Jazz Band and the New Orleans Classic Rag Time Band.

The annual Black Ships Festival, a July spectacular, commemorates Newport-native Commodore Matthew Perry's 1853 expedition that opened the ports of Japan to world trade. Entertainment is also provided throughout the year by a number of local groups, including The Swanhurst Chorus, Island Moving Company, the Newport Navy Choristers, R.I. Stage 3, the Beechwood

The Newport Music Festival has attracted countless artists of international reputation to its annual presentations which take place in several of Newport's famous mansions. Seen in this 1984 photo are Mischa Maisky, cellist; Jean-Philippe Collard, pianist; and Elmer Booze, page turner.

— *John W. Corbett*

Theatre Company, the Newport Children's Playhouse and the Newport Playhouse dinner theater.

The Arts Alliance

In October 1991, about two dozen representatives of arts and cultural organizations gathered to discuss common issues, problems and hopes for the future. From that meeting emerged a non-profit coalition: the Arts and Cultural Alliance of Newport County. The group obtained a first-year grant, for organizing, from the Prince Charitable Trusts, matched by in-kind services from Salve Regina University. With that assistance, the Alliance became a focusing force for regional efforts to develop performance spaces, marketing plans and other ways to involve the arts in Newport County's tourism economy. With membership of more than 200 individual artists and patrons, it is dedicated to improving the region's cultural climate and the status of artists.

On August 25, 1978, an event was held for the benefit of the Newport Cultural Foundation. Tony Award-winning actress Tessie O' Shea performed for a large audience at the Church of the Patriots. The Foundation also was able to award scholarships in 1994.

In May 1993, the first Maritime Arts Festival and Armed Forces Day Celebration took place in the central waterfront area. Artists and craftspeople displayed works ranging from ship models to scrimshaw. A figurehead carver garnered much attention from the crowd, and local performing artists provided free entertainment. The 1994 festival featured an Ocean State Light Opera Company performance of Gilbert & Sullivan's *The Pirates of Penzance*, staged on the deck of the sloop-of-war *Providence*.

Newport County can also boast of more than a dozen art galleries and craft studios. Throughout the year, they regularly feature special exhibits.

On each December 1st during his tenure as mayor of Newport, Humphrey J. Donnelly III officially proclaimed Christmas in Newport by lighting a bonfire in Eisenhower Park. This photograph was taken in 1978.

— *Newport Daily News*

Other Seasonal Events

Many seasonal events came into existence over the past 25 years. Christmas In Newport is a successful month-long festivity of non-commercial events, including the popular Festival of Trees held by area military commands in the large hall of the Naval Underwater Warfare Center. Proceeds are distributed to area charities. Enthusiasts travel annually by motor coach from New York, New Jersey and Pennsylvania to hear the Choir of the Community Baptist Church, which has won praise for its interpretations of seasonal music and spirituals.

Newport's January Film Festival, presenting vintage and unusual films in various mansions, public libraries and theaters, serves as a bridge between Christmas in Newport and the annual Newport Winter Festival: a 10-day January event sponsored in part by Bank of Newport. The latter festival includes fireworks, music, a progressive dinner, teams of Huskies competing for the Winter Festival Trophy, ice carvings by local chefs, walking tours and a children's treasure hunt.

Theaters and Venues

The former Strand Theater, renamed the "Jane Pickens Theater," re-opened as a first-run movie house. It was named for Mrs. William C. Langley, a Newport summer colonist who was the former

Jane Pickens, a popular nightclub entertainer and national radio personality for NBC. The theater, which has the area's only big screen, has a loyal corps of supporters who have done everything possible to keep it operating.

On July 7, 1970, the Portsmouth Summer Theatre opened in a tent setting. In 1979, local Jamestown thespians renovated the old Jamestown Theater. While they managed to present a few plays, and hoped to bring back motion pictures, the building was eventually converted to a mini-mall.

Libraries

Libraries, the backbone of learning, made considerable progress in Newport County. In 1969, the Newport Public Library experienced its first year in a new building. In 1979, the Middletown Public Library moved into a commodious brick building which had served a generation of Navy families as a day-care and recreation center. Redwood Library, which includes a section that was built in 1748 and is the oldest library building in the nation, added a $550,000 climate-controlled vault to protect priceless documents and manuscripts.

On October 18, 1993, a new $140,000 wing of the Jamestown Philomenian Library was dedicated with appropriate ceremonies. The Portsmouth Free Public Library moved into its expanded and renovated building in 1991. That same year, the $8 million McKillop Library at Salve Regina University opened on March 22.

Museums

The Museum of Newport History, one of our city's unique and exciting new attractions, opened in 1993. Providing a comprehensive overview of Newport since its 1639 founding, it includes exhibits devoted to the Native Americans who resided on Aquidneck Island, the prized work of Newport's Colonial artisans, and the city's association with the Navy. Also on display is the famous Franklin Press used to print Newport's second newspaper, the *Newport Mercury*, in 1758. Still published to this day, the *Mercury* is the oldest continuously published newspaper in the nation.

Also in 1993, the Rhode Island Fishermen and Whale Museum began operation in modest quarters. Now relocated in the

The Museum of Newport History, located in the Peter Harrison-designed 1762 Brick Market, brings three-and-a-half centuries of Newport history to life. Seen in this exhibit is the figurehead from the famous auxiliary bark *Aloha*. The 218-foot-long yacht was owned by summer colonist Commodore Arthur Curtiss James.

— *Newport Historical Society (Del Bogart photo)*

Seamen's Church Institute, it is a favorite with the young, who often have the opportunity to talk with working fishermen.

The Naval War College Museum, one of the finest museums devoted to the Naval presence in Newport, opened in 1978. The circa-1820 building was the original college in 1884, and later the Administration Building for the Naval Base. Before 1884, it served as the town's Poor House.

The Museum of Yachting was founded in 1981. The museum, which eventually found quarters in a building at Fort Adams State Park in 1984, is now contemplating a move to a three-story former textile mill on Thames Street.

And, the Sydney L. Wright Museum opened in Jamestown in 1971. It features archeological discoveries from Conanicut Island.

For the Sake of Discussion

The International Berkeley Society was founded in Newport in 1976 by a group interested in Bishop George Berkeley, the great Anglican philosopher. The Society has sponsored several seminars in the Newport area, where philosophers from around the world have presented dissertations on Berkeley and his thoughts.

The Contemporary Civilization Series of public lectures at the Naval War College have brought many internationally known dignitaries to the podium at Spruance Hall, including His Eminence John Cardinal O'Connor, Archbishop of New York; Lee Iacocca, Chairman of Chrysler Corporation; Pulitzer Prize-winning author Herman Wouk; and His Excellency Shaikh Saud Nasir Al-Sabah, Ambassador of the State of Kuwait.

The Museum of Yachting's flagship, ▷ *Shamrock V*, all dressed up with someplace to go. Owned by Sir Thomas Lipton, it was the Royal Ulster Yacht Club's 1930 challenger for the America's Cup. It was the first time an America's Cup race was held off Newport, and successive campaigns to defend the Cup, by the New York Yacht Club, occurred until the Royal Perth Yacht Club's challenger, *Australia II*, won the world's oldest international sporting trophy. The United States won back the Cup in the contest off Fremantle, Australia, in 1987.

— *Over Narragansett Bay & Beyond*

Sporting Events and Activities

The America's Cup

During this quarter of a century, the United States continued to defend the America's Cup off Newport in 1970, 1974, 1977, 1980 and 1983. These races consistently bolstered area trade, including

Ted Turner at the helm of *Courageous*, the successful defender of the 1977 America's Cup.

— *Museum of Yachting (R. P. Foley photo)*

the otherwise-disappointing tourist season of 1980, attracting thousands of visitors from near and far. Many even came from abroad to view the round-robin series to select a challenger and the elimination races that led to the appointment of the defender by the New York Yacht Club.

In 1983, after holding the world's oldest sporting trophy since 1851, the New York Yacht Club lost the Cup to the Royal Perth Yacht Club of Australia. Called "the race of the century," it took the entire seven-race series to determine the winner. After this momentous upset, the United States regained the Cup in Fremantle, Australia, when Dennis Conner's *Stars & Stripes* beat *Kookaburra*, of Australia, thus moving the Cup to San Diego.

During the years the contests were held off Newport

(1930-1983), prospective challengers came from Italy, France, Sweden, Canada, England, Ireland and Australia. When the New York Yacht Club lost the Cup in 1983, that club had defended it 25 times since 1870. The Newport America's Cup tradition lives on, however. The first all-woman crew to sail for the America's Cup, announced for the 1995 contest, will include three Rhode Islanders: Joan Lee Touchette of Newport, Hannah Swett of Jamestown, and Elizabeth Charles of Providence.

Tactical Maneuvers: The Post-Cup Yachting Tradition

Soon after the loss of the America's Cup, Sail Newport, a non-profit organization, was formed. Working with the Rhode Island State Yachting Committee, it has succeeded in its mission to draw the best sailors of the world to Newport.

The 1994 yachting season included the Sail Newport Sailing Festival; the Bank of Newport Memorial Day Regatta; the finish of the Royal Western Double-Handed Transatlantic Race from Plymouth, England; the Newport-to-Bermuda Race; the New York Yacht Club's Sesquicentennial Regatta and annual cruise; and the spectacular Museum of Yachting Heritage Classic. More than 300 skippers, with approximately 1,500 crew members, sailed in the Michelob Newport Regatta.

The Sail Newport youth program brings sailing to the children of Newport County. Corporate sponsorship helps make it possible.

— Stock Newport / Onne Van Der Wal

Throughout the sailing season, numerous events sponsored by the Narragansett Bay Yachting Association and area yacht clubs also fill the lower Bay with sailboats. With events such as the Annapolis-Newport Yacht Race, the Star Atlantic Coast Championship, the Newport-To-Bermuda Race, pre-Olympic regattas and maxi-boat world championships, Newport can still claim the title of "Yachting Capital of the World." For example, the 1987 Volvo Newport Regatta involved 250 boats, 1,000 crew members, nine classes of yachts and two fleets of cruising-class boats.

Other Yachting Milestones

On August 28, 1982, competitors in the first BOC (British Oxygen Corporation) Around-The-World-Alone Race began a 27,000-

mile sail from Newport, with stops at Cape Town, Sydney and Rio de Janeiro, before returning to Newport. Thirty sailors from 12 nations took part in this grueling race. In another BOC contest, Philippe Jeantot, of France, made a record-setting voyage of 134 days, five hours. Newport hosted its most-recent BOC race in 1990-91.

Eighteen physically handicapped sailors assembled early in August 1988 to register for the Shake-a-Leg Regatta. With 21-foot-long sailboats equipped with self-tacking jibs and seats that swing from side-to-side, and the aid of a few able-bodied sailors, the participants enjoyed a week of sailing. Recent studies have resulted in innovations that help paraplegics actively pursue the sport of sailing, including high-placement booms and double riggings that make it easier for the sails to fall.

Golf

The Newport Country Club claims that its Count de Turin Cup is the oldest golfing trophy in the country. Donated in 1898 by Italy's Count de Turin, Prince Victor Emmanuel, it is contested annually through a 36-hole tournament.

Of course, Newport County has other fine courses, such as Wanemetonomy in Middletown; Green Valley, Pocasset and Montaup in Portsmouth; and the Jamestown Country Club. In addition, the former Beavertail Country Club, once requisitioned for World War II purposes, is being considered for restoration. In December 1993, the Portsmouth Town Council granted a permit for the 36-hole Newport National Golf Club, to be shared by the towns of Portsmouth and Middletown. Believed to be one of two 36-hole courses in New England, it is expected to open in 1995.

From 1980 to 1992, an annual senior tournament was held at the Newport Country Club — part of a national circuit of tournaments organized for Professional Golfers' Association (PGA) players who are over the age of 50. Corporate sponsors included Merrill Lynch, *Golf Digest*, Xerox, Amdahl and NYNEX. Sam Snead participated many times, as did Bob Toski, Gene Littler, Julius Boros and Chi Chi Rodriguez, not to mention at least one appearance by Arnold Palmer. On one occasion, Lee Elder burned up the course with a still-to-be-beaten 11-under-par performance.

Tennis

The Newport Casino, site of the prestigious Virginia Slims Hall of Fame Invitational, in 1881 hosted the nation's first tennis tournament. Over the years, spectators have been rewarded by seeing numerous champions play on the Casino's world-famous grass courts — including Bill Tilden, Don Budge, Tony Trabert and Chris Evert.

Prestigious tournaments played here include the 1991 Prudential Securities Grand National Tournament and Davis Cup

John McEnroe sets up a return shot during the 1991 Davis Cup Tournament, held on Centre Court at the Tennis Hall of Fame.

— *Russ Adams Productions Inc.*

matches. In 1994, the Miller Lite Hall of Fame Tennis Championship increased its prize money to $215,000. Proceeds from that tournament benefit the International Tennis Hall of Fame (opened in 1955), part of the Casino complex.

Currently, the Hall is entering its second phase of improvements. Phase I, which cost $1.4 million, included a new grand staircase with a wall of silver trophies and the installation of two climate-controlled vaults. Phase II, to cost about $1 million, will include the restoration of the Casino's library and the installation of a new heating and air-conditioning system. An elevator will be incorporated to provide access for physically handicapped visitors.

A Newport native, James Van Alen, has even affected how the game itself is played. Van Alen, who was instrumental in establishing the Casino as a center of world tennis, devised the Van Alen Simplified Scoring System (VASSS). It was designed to speed up the game and enable more accurate scheduling of matches. The name was changed to the Van Alen Streamlined Scoring System on the occasion of a 1970 professional tennis players' contest that benefited the Hall of Fame.

Fishing

Some of the biggest striped bass ever taken off shore or by boat have been caught off Beavertail Point in Jamestown. Some have tipped the scales to within a shadow of 70 pounds.

In recent years, many champion-size fish have been taken from our waters. These include a 57-pound striped bass from the surf at Little Compton, a 51-pounder caught south of the Melville piers, a 50-pounder snared in the Mount Hope Bridge area, and a 52-pounder that was boated, while trolling off Brenton Reef, by a 14-year-old boy.

The scrappy bluefish also can surprise anglers. A "chopper" caught off Sakonnet Point weighed at 25 pounds, 4 ounces. Another, at 24 pounds, 4 ounces, was caught off Hope Island. Blackfish, or tautog, can run large in our waters, and a joyous fisherman was rewarded in 1993 with a 15-pound, 2-ounce catch, off Ocean Drive.

Fishermen cast into the surf off Brenton Point, on the evening of July 24, 1994.

— *John W. Corbett*

Races, Derbies and Leagues

Countless sporting events take place, year-round, in the area. The International Jumping Derby, one of the finest events of its kind, was held at The Glen, in Portsmouth, during the first half of these past 25 years. The Rolling Rock/Fort Adams 10-Kilometer Road Race attracts hundreds of harriers to compete for cash prizes. In the annual Swim the Bay contest, several hundred swimmers, rowers and spotters help raise thousands of dollars for the environmental organization, Save the Bay.

The Donnelly Sunset League, organized in 1920, is believed to be the oldest, continuous, twilight baseball league in this country. Through the years, hundreds of teams have been sponsored by local businesses, Naval ships, Naval installations, clubs and associations. In 1994, Debbie Stroczynski, the first woman player in league history, took her position as a second-base player for the "Mudville Nine."

Champions, Record Holders and Dignitaries

Many area residents have attained national recognition. On September 22, 1992, Nancy Raposo biked the 17-mile track in Wharton State Forest, near Egg Harbor, New Jersey, setting a world record by riding a 439.65-mile course in 24 hours. In 1993, Newport yachtsman Ken Read was nominated for the Sullivan Award, which recognizes the nation's top amateur athlete. That same year, he won his third consecutive, and fifth overall, J-24 World Championship. Read, the 1985 "Rolex Yachtsman of The Year," has also won such events as the J-24 North American, the Columbus Cup and Antigua Race Week. Claire Ferguson of Jamestown progressed through a number of positions with the United States Figure Skating Association, including Olympic Judge and Olympic World Team Leader, to become the first woman president for this governing body.

Championship Teams

When Rogers High School observed its centennial in 1973, there were additional reasons for jubilation: the school won State championships in both baseball and girls' cross-country. The Newport Rugby Club, formed in 1980, made a clean sweep, in 1989, on a Caribbean trip, defeating a British team in the British Virgin Islands and an American team at St. John, U.S. Virgin Islands. The team had also traveled to Ireland and Nova Scotia. And, the Salve Regina University men's basketball team claimed the Commonwealth Coast Conference Championship held in Boston in 1989.

The area's private schools, St. George's (in Middletown), Portsmouth Abbey and the Naval Academy Prep School, participate in numerous sports, including lacrosse, hockey, field hockey and soccer.

Other Sports and Diversions

The Newport sporting tradition is about as varied as you'll find anywhere. Individuals have popularized such activities as surfing, windboard sailing and, during the winter, "frostbite sailing." Jet-skiers first appeared in our waters in 1988. Polo, which dates back to 1876, is beginning to enjoy a revival on the island, with teams participating in the Newport International Polo Series.

Croquet, that "vicious" game played in serene settings,

Sylvia Moser and Joan McNulty, of Toronto, determining the best way to go with their game of croquet at the Newport Casino, 1989.

— *Newport Daily News*

regained popularity about 12 years ago. From May 24 to 31, 1992, the U.S. Croquet Association hosted the World Croquet Championship at the Newport Casino. Contestants from 10 countries participated. During July of 1994, the United States Croquet Association held its New England Regional Championships at the Newport Casino, and will be hosting the National Singles, Doubles and Seniors Championship there, from September 19 to 25. The Croquet Hall of Fame was opened recently at the Newport Art Museum.

Jai alai, a fast and thrilling professional sport, made its Newport debut on June 10, 1976, at the specially built $6.5 million Newport Fronton. Played in Spain for centuries, jai alai is known to the Basques as *pelota vasca*, which translates to "merry festival." In mid-September 1992, video gambling also opened at the fronton, with $37,000 wagered the first day. With state approval of "Keno" in 1993, slot-like games were added.

Preservation, Restoration and Redevelopment

The Preservation Society of Newport County

The Preservation Society of Newport County experienced growth from 1969 to 1971, starting with the 1969 acquisition of "Chateau-Sur-Mer," an outstanding example of Victorian architecture, dating from 1852.

The Society acquired four more properties in 1971. "Kingscote," built in 1839, in the "romantic Gothic" style, is considered the first summer cottage built in the United States. It was erected for the George Noble Jones family of Savannah. "Rosecliff," a McKim, Mead and White-designed villa, built in 1901, is modeled after the Grand Trianon at Versailles. The "Green Animals" exhibit in Portsmouth, one of the nation's top three topiary gardens, maintains over 80 sculptured trees and animal-shaped shrubs. In addition, "The Breakers," the Cornelius Vanderbilt mansion that has been open to visitors since 1948, was acquired and has become the principal draw for the Society.

The Society, with the cooperation of Christie's of New York, held its first annual symposium in 1993. Its 1994 symposium, entitled "European and American Drawing Rooms," attracted 250 participants from 23 states, the District of Columbia and three foreign countries.

Bellevue Avenue, long associated with Newport's millionaire summer colony, recently received a $7.5-million facelift that helped the famed street to maintain its stature as one of the world's most beautiful and fashionable streets. The two-and-a-half-year project to restore it to its 1920s appearance included concrete resurfacing, the installation of 200 reproductions of the original streetlamps, new granite curbing and the planting of trees. On June 6, 1992, a dedication parade was held to celebrate the work.

— *Preservation Society of Newport County*

Maintenance of the organization's properties is a constant challenge for the Preservation Society of Newport County. In this 1993 photograph, a craftsman is restoring ceiling mouldings in the ballroom of "Marble House."

— *Preservation Society of Newport County*

The Restoration Catalyst

The greatest strides were made by The Newport Restoration Foundation, established in 1968 by Doris Duke, the late tobacco heiress. When Miss Duke passed away in November 1993, she had restored 83 vintage properties. What were once eyesores, subjected to asbestos coverings and other poor modifications, became exquis-

Since Colonial days, Newport has been famous for its artisans and craftsmen, especially during its "Golden Age" — an era that preceeded the Revolutionary War by three or four decades. It produced the famous Townsend and Goddard furniture makers, several outstanding silversmiths and pewterers, watch and clock makers, as well as master builders.

During the past few decades, many contemporary craftsmen and artisans have been involved in restoration projects. Typical of their work is the 1711 David King House, at 34 Pelham Street, seen here as it appeared in the 1960s and today, after it was rescued by the late Doris Duke's Newport Restoration Foundation. The original doorway had been preserved and was donated by Mrs. Ethel King Russell.

— *Newport Restoration Foundation*

ite examples of the periods in which they were built. With the exception of the Prescott Farm (in Middletown) and the Samuel Whitehorne house, which are open to the public, the properties are leased to tenants.

Miss Duke's family was identified with Newport's summer colony since the turn of the century. Her father, James B. Duke, purchased the former Frederick W. Vanderbilt mansion, "Rough Point," in 1923. Her goal in establishing the foundation was to "preserve and restore the city's historic architecture of the eighteenth and nineteenth centuries."

Although restoration of Colonial dwellings began in the mid-1940s, Miss Duke's massive restoration program is considered the catalyst for the restoration of many more privately owned houses. Queen Anne Square, the green which fronts Trinity Church, was also one of Miss Duke's projects; it was dedicated by Queen Elizabeth II, in 1976. Today, visitors can walk Newport's streets and view the work that serves as a memorial to her foresight.

Other Restorations

In 1968, Trinity Church was designated a National Historic Landmark by the United States Department of the Interior. In 1985, a successful drive to raise $2.5 million from corporate sponsors, private donors and Trinitarians resulted in saving from demolition the beautiful 1726-built meeting house.

Newport's 1762-built Brick Market, designed by Peter Harrison, underwent preservation and restoration, at a cost of $1.2 million, of which $600,000 was a grant from the National Endowment for the Humanities; fund-raising activities by the Newport Historical Society brought in another half-million. The latter amount paid for the design and construction of displays for the Museum of Newport History, which opened in 1993.

The recently restored Rose Island Lighthouse provided the best vantage point from which to view the 1992 "Parade of Sail."

— *Rose Island Lighhouse Foundation*

On October 24, 1985, the Rose Island Lighthouse Foundation opened membership to raise $40,000 for initial restoration work on the abandoned Rose Island Lighthouse. As of this writing, $500,000 in cash, and an equal amount in contributed services from local craftspeople, has been expended to restore the lighthouse to its original 1869-70 appearance. Paying guests are now welcome to stay in this unusual bed-and-breakfast locale.

Redevelopment

Newport's downtown-redevelopment program began in 1967 with the demolition of old buildings, including some good ones. Traffic flow in the downtown area was opened up considerably by a new four-lane waterside road, America's Cup Avenue. Many mixed-use structures, with retail shops on the ground floors and apartments above, were built.

The most extensive project took place on Goat Island, where torpedoes were once made for the Navy. Destroyer piers were transformed into a marina, and a hotel went up on the north end — the first new hotel in Newport in a half-century.

Other hotels and motels soon sprang up in the city and outlying island communities. Bed-and-breakfast accommodations, after a slow start in the 1970s, mushroomed in the 1980s. Visitors can now take rooms in former mansions once owned by millionaires, in restored Colonial or Victorian houses, or in smaller comfortable dwellings.

Redevelopment projects of all types surfaced regularly throughout the city. In 1980, for example, Newport's City Council amended a zoning ordinance to permit redevelopment of the former Paramount Theater into housing for the elderly and handicapped. During the summer of 1988, the $3.2 million final phase of the Tonomy Hill renovation replaced streets and sidewalks in the housing project. Renovations were also planned for other Newport Housing Authority properties, including the adjoining Park Holm project.

Land Acquisition

In 1972, the Town Of Portsmouth made a most significant acquisition of land when it purchased about 75 acres of "The Glen," the former estate of Moses Taylor, which overlooks the Sakonnet River. In 1989, the Town purchased an additional 95 acres, abutting the original purchase.

Today, the beautiful 1923-built "Glen Manor House," designed by John Russell Pope, is rented by local organizations and private parties for functions such as the annual Christmas-season "Holly Ball." Several of the spacious rooms in this 31-room replica of a French chateau appeared in the motion picture, "The Great Gatsby." The property's open fields have provided the setting for various festivals, sporting events and outdoor gatherings, including the once-popular International Jumping Derby. With a large boathouse and pier, it is a recreation area that would be hard to duplicate.

In 1977, an organization known as Camelot Gardens, Inc., purchased a considerable part of "Hammersmith Farm," on Ocean Drive, the estate of the late Hugh D. Auchincloss, stepfather of Jacqueline Bouvier Kennedy Onassis. Used as a "Summer White House" during the Kennedy administration, it was opened to the public on May 1, 1978.

In honor of Portsmouth's observance of the 1976 national bicentennial, the United States General Services Administration gave the Town a present: sufficient acreage to develop a campground and recreation area in the town's Melville section.

In 1981, the property of the late Thomas Carr Watson, known as Jamestown's gentleman farmer, was acquired by the Society for the Preservation of New England Antiquities. The Society continues to maintain it as an operating farm, which is open to visitors.

Middletown added to its parks system with the 1993 dedication of Paradise Park. That same year, its Town Council allocated $50,000 which is to be used to move the Boyd Windmill from Portsmouth. As part of its 1994 Arbor Day program, Middletown dedicated "Albro Woods," a treed preserve on Mitchell's Lane.

Heritage

The city's Religious Heritage Weekend, established in 1994, seems destined to become a springtime highlight. In its early days, Newport was a haven for the religiously oppressed — as was the entire colony of Rhode Island. As a result, Quaker, Jewish, Moravian, Huguenot, Baptist, Episcopalian and Congregationalist sects all established roots here. As one may expect in a seaside trading port, Newport has also attracted people of diverse backgrounds.

The United States' oldest Jewish house of worship, Touro Synagogue, was commemorated on August 22, 1982, with the issue of a Postal Service stamp.

Black History Month has long been an important observance in the area. In 1994, it took on added significance when West Broadway was renamed Dr. Marcus F. Wheatland Boulevard. The Barbados-born Dr. Wheatland was the first black physician to practice on Aquidneck Island. After serving on a British ship from 1884 to 1887, he arrived at Boston, both poor and sick. Wheatland eventually attended evening schools and became a physician. A pioneer in radiology, possibly one of the first to use an X-ray machine, he served as president of the National Medical Association and was a member of Newport Hospital's staff.

Irish Festival Month, held during March, originated in 1977. Lectures about Irish history and culture and music are stressed as part of a celebration that kicks off with a big parade on or around St. Patrick's Day.

Newport and the Navy

In 1946, Newport was designated to be a home port for 100 ships. By 1973, only 43 ships were based here and the downsizing of

The full impact of the use of Piers I and II at the Naval Education and Training Center is shown here, circa 1973, with 43 ships in port.

— © John T. Hopf

Naval installations was imminent: a move that would eventually take away the ships.

The Officer Candidate School

The Navy's Officer Candidate School (OCS) was established here in 1951. Amazingly, within its first 10 years, it had commissioned more officers than the United States Naval Academy had since its founding in 1845. In all, the OCS graduated 100,573 during its 42 years at Newport.

The school's graduates include many who attained the rank of captain and admiral, including Admiral Jeremy Michael Boorda (also a University of Rhode Island graduate), who became chief of Naval operations in 1994. One officer candidate who was already well-known when he reported to the school was David Eisenhower, grandson of President Eisenhower. The first female graduate of the school was commissioned on November 2, 1973.

The school's Pass-In-Review ceremonies attracted many visitors, especially with the large classes of its first 20 years. On October 16, 1993, county residents were shocked to learn that the OCS was to be consolidated with the Aviation Officer Candidate School in Pensacola, Florida.

The Naval Downsizing

On December 1, 1971, it was learned that a Naval Reserve program was to begin with the assignment of four destroyers to Newport. The good news was rather short-lived. On April 16, 1973 — a date long remembered in the area — it was announced that all the Navy installations would be closed (except the complex of schools, the Naval War College and the Naval Underwater Systems Center — later renamed the Naval Underwater Warfare Center), and that the fleet was to be removed from Newport.

The closing of the Quonset Naval Air Station on the west side of Narragansett Bay, where 3,400 civilians and 4,300 military were employed, was particularly devastating. Between the Newport and Quonset closings, it was estimated that the military population of 16,000 would be reduced to 2,600 by July 1, 1974. Rhode Island would account for 51% of the total loss of military personnel involved in the nationwide downsizing.

On April 18, area leaders began to assess the loss and prepare for the future. There was hope that the ballistic support pier at Melville, on standby status since its completion, would become a base for Trident submarines. The State established an Office of Economic Renewal to aid businesses faced with financial problems. A task force was formed to deal with surplus property that the Navy would release. The Newport County Chamber of Commerce convened a special directors' meeting to seek answers. Concern ran deep enough to move hundreds to lead a "Save Our Ships" march in Washington, D.C.

New Hope on the Horizon

A little less than a year after the Naval downsizing, there were positive signs that Newport would remain a vital part of the Navy's

15 Ships Return To City

Fifteen ships of the Navy's Cruiser-Destroyer Force, Atlantic, will return to Newport in time for the Christmas holidays from extended operations around the world.

The ships have been in combat operations off Vietnam and in peaceful operations in the Indian Ocean, near South America and in the Mediterranean.

"The returning ships are the guided missile frigates Dewey, Farragut and Luce, guided missile escorts Furer and Talbot, destroyers Basilone, Davis, J.P. Kennedy, Forrest Sherman and Brownson, ocean escorts Koelsch, Voge, Bowen, Joseph Hewes and Trippe.

The Navy has announced that 30 of 42 ships homeported in Newport will be here for the holiday.

This typical news item appeared on December 1, 1972 — just four months prior to the announcement that the Navy fleet would be leaving Newport.

— *Newport Daily News*

training program. Overall, Newport has managed to maintain considerable ties with the Navy, despite the whims of politics, reduced defense budgets and the passing of the Cold War era.

The Naval Base, Naval Station and the Naval Officer Training Center were consolidated into the newly formed Naval Education and Training Center (NETC), on March 29, 1974. The first contingent of 2,458 midshipmen arrived in May, of that year, for summer training.

The Naval Academy Preparatory School was moved from Bainbridge, Maryland, back to Newport, its 1915 birthplace. Its mission was to prepare diverse enlisted members of the active-duty fleet, and reserves from the Navy, Marine Corps and Coast Guard, for the Academy.

On December 12, 1984, two new guided missile frigates, the *USS Simpson* and the *USS Samuel B. Roberts*, were assigned to Newport. It was estimated their presence annually would add more than $3.5 million to the area economy. It would also bring a $3 million renovation of Pier II and the rehabilitation of the abandoned Anchorage Navy housing in Middletown.

In December 1989, the *USS Normandy*, a guided missile Aegis-class cruiser, was brought to Newport for her commission-

The *USS Rhode Island*, the fifteenth of 18 Trident submarines built for the Navy, passes by Fort Adams as it enters Narragansett Bay on June 30, 1994.

— *Newport Daily News*

ing. On July 9, 1994, area residents celebrated another commissioning, of the Trident sub *USS Rhode Island*, at Pier II.

The Naval War College

The Naval War College, established in 1884, was often threatened with extinction during its career. Yet, even during the "doom and gloom" era of the 1970s, the college saw physical expansion, including the construction of Hewitt Hall, Spruance Hall and Conolly Hall.

Accordingly, the Naval War College has grown from a few hundred personnel to more than 1,000. Its goals are to enhance the command and management capabilities of senior and mid-career officer/students, and to develop advanced strategic and tactical concepts for future deployment by Naval forces.

The Naval Underwater Warfare Center has also endured, despite the overall downsizing at NETC. Ground was broken on January 20, 1994, for an $11.2-million Submarine Electromagnetic Systems Laboratory which will serve as the Navy's principal research facility for submarine communication, electronic warfare, electro-optics and periscope systems. Ground will be broken for another building in 1994, to cost $21 million. This 200,000-square-foot facility will serve as the Undersea Acoustics Research and Development Laboratory.

The Second Downsizing

With the 1993 downsizing of national military installations, the last of a dozen ships assigned to Newport were transferred or disposed of. For the first time in more than a century, Newport was without an assigned ship.

Vice Admiral Robert K. U. Kihune, chief of Naval education and training, brought good news during his March 1994 visit. Admiral Kihune announced the NETC's Senior Enlisted Academy would be transformed into a school for prospective command master chiefs — the chiefs who serve as top enlisted personnel. At some time during fiscal 1995, a leadership training course for prospective commanding officers is to be implemented. It will bring to the installation those who have attained the rank of commander and captain. Part of the reason to locate both ranks at NETC, according to the admiral, is to encourage interaction between the two — "interaction that is mirrored in real life in the fleet."

The *USS Newport* (LST-1179), one of 20 "Newport Class" tank-landing ships, was commissioned at Philadelphia, on June 7, 1969. The 522-foot ship (561-foot, including derrick arms) was christened by Nuala Pell, wife of Senator Claiborne Pell. The *Newport* made a first visit to her namesake city on August 4, 1970; more than 800 people toured her that day. The big ship made subsequent Newport visits, the last of which was in July 1992. Two months later, the *Newport* was decommissioned at Norfolk, and her ship's bell was presented to the City of Newport.

— *United States Navy*

Tourism and Attractions

Since 1969, the year the Newport Bridge was completed, much has been done to enhance the area's tourist industry. With the reduction of the military presence, Newport leadership finally recognized that tourism offered a major economic opportunity. (In 1946, about 20 motor-coach tours came to Newport; as a result of our increased emphasis on tourism, that number reached more than 3,000 in 1993.) The greatest boon was the opening to the public of

Since 1962, modern cruise ships have been making port calls in Narragansett Bay. By 1980, Newport began to be a regular port of call. Today, Newport averages 30 such visits per season, with ships arriving from May to October. Shown above is the magnificent *Queen Elizabeth 2*, which has made many visits. Trinity Church's steeple is in the foreground.

— *Newport Daily News*

several mansions owned by the Preservation Society of Newport, including "Belcourt Castle," "Hammersmith Farm" and "Beechwood." However, the road to building a tourist industry has not always been a smooth one.

The oil embargo, brought about by the actions of the Organization of Petroleum Exporting Countries (OPEC) during the early 1970s, affected New England business, in general, and the tourist industry, in particular. At that time, the State ran newspaper advertisements in out-of-state newspapers that proclaimed Rhode Island was only "4 gallons long, 3 gallons wide." It must have worked. While tourism in many New England areas dropped by as much as 40%, Rhode Island suffered only about a 20% drop in tourist revenue.

Current Attractions

On June 8, 1988, the multi-million dollar Gateway Transportation and Visitors Center opened. Financed through a combination of Federal, State and City funds, it provides visitor information and parking docks for motor coach tours. The close proximity of the Old Colony & Newport Railroad, a tourist rail system, completes a unique complex.

Harbor and motor-coach tours of the city and waterfront, which are fast becoming major attractions, provide narrated overviews of the city that enable visitors to "zero in" on places they'd most like to visit. Information on such sites and walking tours of the historic center-city area are graciously provided by the Newport County Convention and Visitors' Bureau.

The Newport County Railroad Foundation, later to become the National Railroad Foundation, "reorganized" the Old Colony & Newport Railroad in 1979. Its first piece of rolling stock was a 1927 Brill motor coach and parlor car. The railroad runs a scenic tourist route from Long Wharf to "Green Animals" Topiary Garden in Portsmouth. Visitors continue to patronize this tourist train, which runs for several miles along Narragansett Bay.

The *Newport Star Clipper*, a dinner train, made its initial run in October 1988. It utilizes the State-owned tracks, over which the Old Colony & Newport Railroad operates. The train also arranges special luncheon runs.

The Gateway Transportation and Visitors Center, on America's Cup Avenue, opened on June 8, 1988. The headquarters of the Newport County Convention and Visitors Bureau, it is across the street from the terminal of the Old Colony & Newport Railway, which passes the Naval Education and Training Center and scenic vistas of Narragansett Bay.

— *Newport County Convention & Visitors Bureau*

The *H.M.S. Rose* and Classic Yachts

The replica of the British Revolutionary War frigate *HMS Rose*, considered the first major waterfront attraction, was opened to visitors on July 13, 1970. Since moving to Bridgeport, Connecticut, in 1987, it frequently returns to Newport to participate in patriotic exercises. In 1971, the 125-foot schooner *Bill of Rights*, modeled after an 1850 contraband runner, was based for a few years in Newport for charter and cruising purposes.

Today, visitors are able to cruise aboard two of the three remaining America's Cup "J" boats — the *Shamrock V*, now the flagship of the Museum of Yachting, and the newly-restored *Endeavour*, which contested for the America's Cup in 1930 and 1934, respectively. This class of yacht measured from 120 to 135 feet in length, with masts as tall as a 16-story building. Also based in Newport

Seen here beneath the Pell Bridge, *Shamrock V*, (right) the first "J" boat to challenge for the America's Cup, in 1930, and *Endeavour*, (left) unsuccessful challenger in 1934, are now part of the Newport scene. *Shamrock V* is the Museum of Yachting's flagship.

— *Providence Journal-Bulletin*

for charter and day cruises are 12-meter yachts (62 to 68 feet long) used in the Cup races between 1958 and 1987.

Developments on "The Drive"

In October 1993, a contract for improvements at Fort Adams State Park was awarded by the Army Corps of Engineers. Plans include a second-floor wooden walkway that will provide a spectacular view of lower Narragansett Bay and Newport Harbor. The fort, the second-largest built in this country, serves as the operating base for Sail Newport and the present Museum of Yachting. With open fields for outdoor sports and a beach, it is also the location of both the JVC Jazz Festival and the Ben & Jerry's Newport Folk Festival.

A memorial to Portuguese navigators was dedicated on June 25, 1989, at Brenton Point State Park. Perhaps the most spectacular monument erected in Newport County, it consists of several stone pillars with a huge, stone compass rose as its centerpiece. A Fishermen's Memorial is to be erected, in the near future, at the park.

The Bicentennial and Patriotic Events

For such a small area, the Newport region celebrated the nation's 1976 bicentennial in a very big way. Highlights included a week-long visit of the "Tall Ships," 16 of which arrived in June, via the Bermuda-to-Newport race. From vantage points along the bay, a crowd estimated at 100,000 witnessed the "Parade of Sail." Norway's Crown Prince Harald and his wife, Princess Sonja, attended the program's awards ceremony on the eve of June 30, prior to the ships' departure for a July 4th celebration in New York.

Chile's *Esmeralda*, left, and Russia's big four-masted *Kruzenshtern* head for positions in the "Parade of Sail," July 1, 1976.

— *Newport Daily News*

As part of the State's bicentennial observance, "Seaport '76" built a replica of the sloop *Katy*, which served as the Rhode Island Navy in 1775. (The original *Katy* was later called to Philadelphia, to become the first ship of the Continental Navy, and was renamed *Providence*.)

Other Bicentennial Visitors

On July 7, the French destroyer *Duperre* and the anti-submarine corvette *Drogue* arrived for a five-day visit as part of France's observance of our bicentennial. Their presence recalled the 1780 arrival of General Count de Rochambeau and his 6,000 troops that occupied Newport prior to the march to Yorktown. On July 8, French Ambassador Jacques Kosciusko-Morizet was a guest of honor at a reception held at Fort Adams. He presented a bust of French Admiral Pierre André de Suffren, who participated in a 1778 no-win battle with a British fleet. Governor Philip Noel presented the ambassador with a cannon from a scuttled British warship.

The French destroyer *Duperre*, arriving in Newport on July 7, 1976, in the course of a United States Bicentennial visit to East Coast ports. She was accompanied by the anti-submarine corvette *Drogue*. The French ambassador hosted a reception, that evening, aboard the *Duperre*.

— *Newport Daily News*

On July 10, at 6:35 P.M., Queen Elizabeth II arrived by limousine at Trinity Church, accompanied by Prince Philip, the Duke of Edinburgh, and by Governor and Mrs. Philip W. Noel. Applauded along the city route, the queen was enthusiastically greeted at the church. While here, the queen unveiled a plaque officially designating the large landscaped area west of Trinity Church

Queen Elizabeth II is greeted by Reverend Charles J. Minifie, on the occasion of her United States Bicentennial visit to Trinity Church, where she dedicated Queen Anne Square. Prince Philip and Mayor Humphrey J. Donnelley III are at center of photograph.

— *Providence Journal-Bulletin*

as "Queen Anne Square." About a half-hour later, the distinguished visitors arrived at the Navy piers where the royal yacht *Britannia* was docked.

The queen's dinner guests that evening included President and Mrs. Gerald R. Ford, Vice President and Mrs. Nelson A. Rockefeller, Secretary of State and Mrs. Henry Kissinger, Secretary of Commerce and Mrs. Elliot Richardson, U.S. Senator and Mrs. Claiborne Pell, Governor and Mrs. Noel and U.S. Ambassador to Great Britain Anne Armstrong, accompanied by her husband.

Civic Anniversaries

Portsmouth's 350th birthday was highlighted in 1988 by the presence of the frigate *Rose* which "bombarded" the beach at Island Park. In 1989, on May 4, the City of Newport began its 350th anniversary festivities with a ceremony at the Colony House, followed by a big parade on the 7th. A 350th-birthday capsule was buried in front of City Hall. In addition, a huge floral bed was planted in Eisenhower Park in the shape and colors of a pineapple, a longtime symbol of hospitality that has been identified with Newport for more than 250 years. Middletown observed its 250th birthday in May 1993. On the 15th, a parade featured, among other things, a Mummers band from Philadelphia and a U.S. Postal Service float, introducing the town's new Zip Code. The Town of Tiverton celebrated its 300th birthday in 1994.

More Historic Events

Many area festivals are patriotic in nature. On August 26, 1978, the bicentennial of the Battle of Rhode Island was duly observed when 1,700 combatants re-enacted the battle at Lehigh Hill, Portsmouth. The combatants represented Colonial militia and British and Hessian units. In the morning, a brigade of highly trained British units marched through the streets of Newport, took up their positions, and engaged in a very realistic mock battle with the militia and Continentals.

Simultaneously, the frigate *Rose* and the Continental sloop-of-war *Providence* "did battle" on the bay, in sight of the land action. The next day, Major General Julius W. Becton, Jr., commander of the U.S. Operational Test and Evaluation Agency, spoke at the Black Regiment Memorial in Portsmouth, a short walk from Lehigh Hill. It was the bicentennial of a notable battle on August 29, 1778, at which the first organized regiment of blacks and Indians fought with great courage and embarrassed the fierce-looking Hessians by repulsing them *three* times.

Continuing a Tradition of Research

In February 1994, the Rhode Island Historical Preservation Commission awarded two grants to the City of Newport. The first grant, for $6,000, was to search underwater sites in Narragansett Bay for historic artifacts. The second, for $3,000, enabled the Newport Common Burial Ground Advisory Committee to survey and photograph all existing markers in the Common Burial Ground.

Getting Along Famously

Perhaps no other community our size has hosted so many distinguished visitors. For various official and personal reasons, we have been visited by heads of state, stars of the entertainment world, high-ranking military personnel, cabinet officials and noted artists.

Distinguished Visitors

President Richard M. Nixon visited Newport on at least three occasions. In March 1971, Nixon attended the graduation of his son-in-law, David Eisenhower, at the Officer Candidate School. In August 1980, former President Nixon took a cruise on the Newport yacht *Star Mist* with his friend "Bebe" Rebozo. Nixon's successor, Gerald Ford, also visited here on at least three occasions, in 1960, 1975 and 1976.

Vice President George Bush came to meet the crew of the yacht chosen to defend the America's Cup — one of two visits he made here. Bush once trained at the Naval Auxiliary Airfield in Charlestown. His grandfather, father and a nephew were graduates of St. George's School in Middletown.

Vice President Nguyen Cao Ky and Mme. Ky, of South Vietnam, visited the Naval War College in 1970, and Mme. Ky took time to visit some of the area's historic attractions. Crown Prince Harald and Princess Sonja, of Norway, attended the Tall Ships Ball in 1976. King Hussein, of Jordan, after attending the Brown University graduation of his son, spent a few days in Newport. Sweden's King Gustav XVI and Queen Silvia spent several mid-August days in 1980 viewing the trial races of Sweden's entry as a challenger for the America's Cup. President Alfredo Cristiani, of El Salvador, was at Portsmouth Abbey on the occasion of his son's graduation.

Prime Minister Robert Hawke, of Australia, made a visit to the Australian yachtsmen to wish them well in the 1983 Cup contest — which they won. Crown Prince Hans Liechtenstein, of Liechtenstein, visited in July 1984. Princess Margaret, Prince Edward and Prince Andrew, of Great Britain, were here on separate

Nelson Aldrich Rockefeller, whose mother was a Providence native, made numerous visits to Rhode Island. He came to Newport, in 1972, while he was governor of New York.

On May 23, 1976, Vice President Rockefeller delivered an address to the members of the Touro Synagogue. As part of the program, Metropolitan Opera soprano Roberta Peters sang the national anthem.

— *Newport Daily News*

134

visits. Mme. Georges Pompidou, widow of the President of France, visited in 1986. Bishop Desmond Tutu, of South Africa, was a recent visitor.

Cabinet members such as Secretary of the Navy John Lehman and Secretary of the Interior Donald P. Hodel were among us, too. General P. X. Kelly, commandant of the Marine Corps, and General William C. Westmoreland were among the numerous military visitors.

The Stars Come Out

Over the years, Bob Hope, Frank Sinatra, Victor Borge, Barbra Streisand, Jane Fonda, Anna Moffo, Sid Caesar and Eddie Fisher have entertained us at various events. Jack Lemmon was seen at the 1981 Newport Country Club 36-hole, two-ball, best-ball tournament. Eli Wallach and his wife, Anne Jackson, opened the newly restored Newport Casino Theatre on July 1, 1982, with their presentation of "Bits and Pieces." Dina Merrill served as hostess for the opening night reception.

Artist Andy Warhol served as co-chairman of the International Jumping Derby in 1985. Actor Tab Hunter was on the island to judge a horse show. Charles Bronson and his family attended one of the International Jumping Derby contests.

Other celebrities passing through, visiting friends, enjoying yachting activities or attending functions have included Malcolm Forbes; Stephanie Powers; Robert Wagner; Margaux Hemingway; Christopher Reeve; Buddy Ebsen; Christie Brinkley; Gene Rayburn; Anthony Edwards; Douglas Fairbanks, Jr.; John Forsythe; Burgess Meredith; Carmel Quinn; Ilene Kristen, of the soap opera "Ryan's Hope"; William F. Buckley; Lana Cantrell; January Jones; and Valerie Perrine.

Hollywood Discovers Newport

In 1956, with the assistance of the Preservation Society of Newport County, locations in Newport were used for the filming of *High Society*. The Preservation Society then began a unique marketing campaign designed to attract motion picture and TV producers to consider their properties for film locations. The Preservation Society's promotional efforts have also attracted advertising agencies to use Society properties in print and TV campaigns for a diverse range of products.

Feature films made in Newport include *The Man Without A Country, The Great Gatsby, The Scarlet Letter, The Bostonians, The Kennedys of Massachusetts, Mr. North, True Lies, Wind,* and most recently, *The Buccaneers.* Producers of Public Broadcasting System classics (such as Alistair Cooke's *America, The Adams Chronicles* and *On the Waterways*), along with other networks covering special events, anniversaries and live shows, have found the Newport region ideal for settings.

Sir Laurence Olivier, one of several movie stars on location for the 1977 filming of *The Betsy*, at the wheel of a vintage automobile on the grounds of "The Elms."

— © *Allied Artists Pictures Corp.*

The Preservation Society's promotional efforts have also attracted advertising agencies to use its properties in print and TV campaigns for a diverse range of products. For several years, the State's Department of Economic Development has also played an active role in promoting sites in Newport and throughout the state.

As a result, an impressive list of stars have worked in Newport. The list includes Cliff Robertson, Lauren Bacall, Anjelica Huston, Robert Duvall, Mia Farrow, Bruce Dern, Tommy Lee Jones, Katherine Ross, Robert Mitchum, Robert Redford, Christopher Reeve, Vanessa Redgrave, Arnold Schwarzenegger, Karen Black, Sam Waterston, Robert Ryan, Joseph Wiseman, Cloris Leachman, Lesley-Anne Down, Edward Herrmann and Andy Griffith.

In the summer of 1970, a movie star of a different ilk appeared in Newport. "Coquette," a hot-air balloon featured in the classic motion picture *Around the World in 80 Days,* was here as part of a hot-air-balloon festival at "Chateau-Sur-Mer," sponsored by the Preservation Society and the Newport Music Festival.

The Effects of War Hit Home

In the post-Cold War period, it is not uncommon to see sailors of foreign lands in our city — as when 86 Soviet navymen came here on May 14, 1975. But the past 25 years were not always years of peace, as active and reserve military units were often called upon to participate in areas of unrest.

By far, the most action was seen during the controversial Vietnam War. Combat troops were sent to South Vietnam during

the 1960s and early 1970s to bolster efforts to ward off an invasion by North Vietnamese soldiers. It was not a popular agenda. Protests were staged at the entrance to the Naval Base, and a big rally was held on October 15, 1969, when 700 vented their feelings at Eisenhower Park. Finally, in January 1973, the Vietnam War observed a cease-fire and later that year the United States withdrew its troops.

Many Newport County families were affected by the war, as reflected by the area's several memorials. On the lawn of Newport's City Hall is a memorial to Newporters who lost their lives

Secretary of Navy John H. Chafee is shown greeting a Vietnamese officer candidate, in April 1970, at Newport Navy Base. Chafee served as Rhode Island's governor from 1963 to 1969 and is presently a member of the U.S. Senate.

— *Newport Daily News*

in Vietnam. A 1,700-pound marble block from Vietnam, to which was attached a brass plaque, was placed on display in the Officer Candidate School "Gallery of Heroes" at the Naval Education and Training Center. The plaque lists the names of OCS graduates killed or missing in action in Vietnam.

Other Wartime Incidents

On October 23, 1983, 219 Marines, 18 Navy sailors and four U.S. Army soldiers died in an attack on the Marine Headquarters in Beirut, Lebanon. Nine of the Marines who lost their lives were from Rhode Island — four from Newport County. Memorials to these victims were dedicated at the Portsmouth Historical Society grounds on May 27, 1984, and at Perrotti Park in Newport on November 9, 1986.

The Newport-based guided-missile frigate *Samuel B. Roberts* left here for the Persian Gulf on January 11, 1988. On April 14, a mine blew a large hole in the ship's hull. The crew's prompt action saved the ship from sinking. She arrived back home on July 30 to a hero's welcome, aboard the Dutch heavy-lift vessel *Mighty Servant II*. The ship later underwent $1.8 million in repairs at the Bath Iron Works in Maine.

The newest part of the Cliff Walk ▷ restoration and improvement project was completed in July 1994, along the ocean by "The Breakers" (upper left of photo) and Salve Regina University (upper right).

— © 1994, John T. Hopf

Conserving Our Environment

Save The Bay, an environmental watchdog organization, was established in 1970 to guard against pollution in Narragansett Bay, protect the state's wetlands and preserve Rhode Island's precious shoreline. Its annual meetings have been addressed by conservationists of national repute, including actor Ted Danson and television reporter Garrick Utley. The organization has helped to spawn an environmentalist movement that has benefited our entire state.

For decades, Newport's famed Cliff Walk has experienced erosion and taken the brunt of storms. Restoration and preservation of this National Recreation Trail began in 1971. With the help of Federal, State and local financing, the work continues to this day.

The Newport Friends of the Waterfront was founded in 1982. Its members work diligently to prevent indiscriminate development of precious waterfront property. The organization continues to put pressure on City officials to name "all public streets and rights of way" on the Newport waterfront.

Environmental action is also becoming more evident in the private sector. On January 25, 1994, three Portsmouth families, who wished to see the Sakonnet Passage vista preserved, deeded to the Town a total of eight acres of land at McCorrie Point.

The area's best-known conservation-inspired attraction is the Norman Bird Sanctuary, in Middletown. In 1984, a dam was restored at the sanctuary to protect pond species that were threatened in past years by low water levels. In a similar spirit, the Conanicut Island Spring Bird Count became an annual May event, in 1985. In January 1994, the Department of Environmental Management released a flock of wild turkeys in a secluded Little Compton field — hoping to initiate the successful propagation of the birds.

In October 1988, a handful of concerned Newporters met to discuss Newport's valuable trees, the subject of books and countless print articles. This led to the formation of the Newport Tree Commission and the hiring of the city's first professional arborist in 30 years. In 1991, the National Arbor Day Foundation gave Newport a Tree City USA award, only the second such honor bestowed in Rhode Island. In 1994, the City won the Arbor Day Tree City Growth Award for outstanding progress.

The past 25 years, however, were not without environmental problems. On June 23, 1989, an oil-spill disaster struck lower Narragansett Bay when *World Prodigy*, a 531-foot tanker loaded with No. 2 heating oil, struck a reef or ledge. Hundreds of thousands of gallons of oil fouled much of the shore area, with the Beavertail area of Jamestown bearing the brunt of the spill.

Transportation

In December 1984, bids were opened for the construction of a four-lane span to replace the outdated two-lane Jamestown Bridge. The bridge was to be 7,350 feet long, would rise 135 feet above

Narragansett Bay, and would cost $63.9 million. After countless delays, the bridge — officially named the Jamestown-Verrazzano Bridge — was opened eight years later. On October 17, 1992, over 40,000 people "celebrated" the opening by walking across its span. The bridge's final cost: a whopping $160 million.

Transportation improvements made were not all related to land travel. In 1993, the United States Coast Guard replaced the 30-year-old Brenton Light Tower, at the entrance to Narragansett Bay, with a 12-foot-high lighted buoy. The buoy features an electric horn, a six-mile radio beacon and a flashing strobe light that is visible for up to nine miles. The radio beacon at Beavertail Light is also destined for a power increase in the near future.

The Jamestown-Verrazzano Bridge, which parallels the 1940 Jamestown Bridge, opened to a special celebration on October 17, 1992. Bands played music, ranging from marches to jazz to Dixieland. Many items were sold along the "Bridge-walk," including traditional Rhode Island food, souvenirs (such as tee shirts) and a limited-edition commemorative coin.

— © John T. Hopf

Fishing vessels, at left, and pleasure craft vie for space in crowded Newport Harbor. This photograph was taken on a September morning in 1983.

— *Jacqueline Denning*

Traffic Congestion: an Ongoing Problem

Newport is the state's only major community that is 30 minutes or more from its nearest interstate highway. Alternate methods have frequently been proposed to relieve traffic on Aquidneck Island, as both East Main Road (Route 138) and West Main Road (Route 114) can no longer safely handle increased use.

One answer, many believe, is to redevelop the Old Colony & Newport Railway. An upgrading of tracks could take passengers to the Heritage Park area of Fall River. It has also been learned that Massachusetts is interested in making the line run to Boston. According to a Commuter and Tourist Railroad Commission study, there is one stumbling block: the need to repair the railroad bridge that connects Portsmouth and Tiverton.

Business, Industry and Commerce

During the mid-1970s, the Aquidneck Corporate Park, in Middletown, became home to many defense contractors. Newport Corporate Park, Enterprise Center and Portsmouth Industrial Park, all developed in the mid-1980s, continued to accommodate the growth in the defense industry.

Grant Plaza (now the Newport Mall) was constructed in 1970. It has reflected the ups and downs of the area's retail buying power. It has had empty stores, from time to time, but as of spring 1994, had leased just about all its space. In 1976, E. Patrick Rooney, president of J. T. O'Connell Inc., announced the purchase of 24 acres of land on West Main Road, in Middletown, which was developed into another large shopping center. Retail interests continue to look upon county communities for new customers, as towns report population growth.

In 1988, at the peak of Navy research and development activities in Newport, the Newport County Chamber of Commerce initiated the Aquidneck 2000 Program, with local business community funding of $250,000, to address community concerns about quality of life and economic diversification. Land-use planning tools, such as the Aquidneck Island Geographic Information System, a Build-Out Analyses Project and the Aquidneck Island Land Trust, were established. In 1989, to meet State-mandated comprehensive planning, the Chamber of Commerce created the Aquidneck Foundation, a non-profit, tax-exempt community organization. The Foundation established a growth-management program, in cooperation with the three Aquidneck Island municipalities and the Conservation Foundation.

When the Berlin Wall fell in November 1989, the Chamber of Commerce created the Aquidneck 2000 Economic Innovation Task Force to develop a model for defense-business diversification and economic revitalization. The Economic Innovation Center (EIC) initiated a long-term sustainable-development strategy, based on human-resource development, emerging-business development and international commerce.

The repeal of the State's marine-related luxury tax has positioned marine-oriented business for growth. Entrepreneurs such as Ted Hood, Everett Pearson and Joel Kane have led, by

Aerial view of Hood Enterprises/
Little Harbor Marine, taken in the
spring of 1994, shows this thriving
Portsmouth business center.

— *Matt Weaver*

Workers at Little Harbor Marine
adjust the propeller on one of the
many yachts built there.

— *Matt Weaver*

example, the chance to seize opportunities along the island's extensive industrial waterfront. In 1978, the transfer of 30 acres of former Navy land, at the Melville section of Portsmouth, lead to the development of Little Harbor Marina, a comprehensive marine-service facility owned and operated by Hood. The marina has recently complied with permit requirements that will allow it to expand into a 1,500-slip marina, as the market demands. The former Weyerhaeuser lumber port is being redeveloped by Kane as the state's newest commercial marine facility. Also in Portsmouth, TPI Inc., owned by Pearson and John Walton, employs 130 workers, hired in 1994, to manufacture giant windmill blades.

Typical of good news in business and industry was the relocation from Massachusetts to Tiverton, in 1993, of JM Engineering, the sole manufacturer of computer-operated textile dyeing machines. The company has found a market in textile plants in North and South Carolina, Georgia, Mexico, Canada, Argentina and Pakistan. Raytheon, long-established in Portsmouth, has kept busy with defense contracts. Today, the area's economic vitality continues to rely upon tourism and defense- and high-tech-related activities.

Weathering the Storms

Mother Nature has thrown us a few punches during the past 25 years. On Monday morning, February 6, 1978, Rhode Islanders started their day, unaware that a major snowstorm was in the mak-

The "Blizzard of '78" caused residents of the Newport area to be snowbound for two days. Providence was hit even harder, and traffic did not move for a week. In this photograph, the Newport Casino is partially hidden by snow plowed from the adjacent shopping plaza's parking lot.

— © 1978 John T. Hopf

ing. By mid-afternoon, the rapid accumulation made it prudent to close schools, businesses and civil and government services. For two full days, it snowed. Reports vary as to the depth of snow on Aquidneck Island — from 16 inches to more than 2 feet, with drifts up to 5 feet. Woonsocket, in the northern part of the state, recorded 54 inches of snow.

During "The Blizzard of '78," it was estimated that more than 30,000 assorted vehicles were abandoned on state and community highways. Newporters enjoyed walking almost-traffic-free streets for several days, and some who needed to get to their places of employment became adept at cross-country skiing.

On September 26, 1985, weather bureaus announced that "the area was looking down a gun barrel." Hurricane Gloria was packing winds of 156 miles per hour as it raced up the East Coast. By the time it reached our area, wind speed had dropped to 77 miles per hour. Luckily, Gloria passed through with a glancing blow, instead of a disastrous head-on encounter.

However, electrical power was lost for 26,000 customers,

boats were blown ashore and trees took a pounding. It was reported that 900 area residents evacuated their shore-exposed properties, taking to the nine emergency shelters that were opened.

On August 19, 1991, Hurricane Bob arrived with ample advance warning, causing the closing of the Pell, Jamestown-Verrazzano and Mount Hope Bridges. Naval ships left their berths to head out to sea to ride out the storm. Easton's Beach, Bailey's

Sections of seawall, sand and boulders from Easton's Beach were strewn across Memorial Boulevard by Hurricane Bob. Hundreds of people came the next day to view the effect of the storm's fury.

— *Newport Daily News*

Beach and others were soon in ruins, as winds of 105 miles per hour drove angry seas against our waterfront areas. Downtown Newport was flooded. Trees were downed and boats were driven ashore.

Out-of-state and Canadian crews arrived to help restore electric power, which was out for most customers for about a week. Tourists left their hotels, but about 200, it was said, took temporary shelter at Rogers High School. About 200 Portsmouth inhabitants took refuge in that Town's high school, as well.

Most recent was the brutal winter of 1993-94. For several weeks before Christmas, there were those hoping for a "White Christmas." Snow started arriving on December 26. By March 19, at least 16 snowfalls were reported. January and February saw snowfalls of up to 10 inches, including back-to-back snowfalls that left a combined total of about 22 inches over one three-day period. Tiverton reported a four-day fall of 21 inches during the second week of February. Cold weather persisted through March.

Et Cetera

Since 1969, Newport County's police stations were either replaced or improved. Tiverton built a station handy to Route 24, in 1977. Newport's force moved out of the 1772-built, former Colony prison into a new $2.5-million structure, in 1984. Middletown added to its station that same year. Jamestown built an attractive new police headquarters, in 1991.

Miantonomi Memorial Park and its McKim, Mead & White-designed World War I memorial tower was designated a National Historic Place on June 23, 1969.

On October 13, 1969, the Right Reverend Don Matthew Stark was consecrated as abbot of the newly designated Portsmouth Abbey, formerly known for 51 years as the Portsmouth Priory.

The eight-story Tower Building of the Newport Hospital was dedicated on August 16, 1970. Costing $7.5 million, ground was broken in August 1967, six years prior to the hospital's centennial.

In 1970, a Newport girl had the distinction of being the first female student at St. George's School, in Middletown.

Ground was broken, in 1973, for a new YMCA of Newport County, on the former Charity Farm, in Middletown. On May 13, 1987, $4.5-million plans were approved for the Church-Community Housing Corporation to buy the former Navy YMCA and convert its 115 dormitory-style rooms into low-cost housing.

Jamestowners elected a charter commission in 1973; Portsmouth approved a home rule charter in 1974, and on October 26, 1992, Portsmouth's Town Council narrowly approved a Comprehensive Community Plan.

In 1974, 85 replica gas lamps were erected to illuminate the historic downtown area of Newport. The first lamp was installed, fittingly, on Pelham Street — where the first gas-illuminated streetlamp in the nation was exhibited in 1806.

The U.S. Coast Guard cutter *Ida Lewis*, currently under construction at Marinette, Wisconsin, is scheduled for commission in 1996. Named for the Newport heroine of the Lime Rock Light, the $22 million craft is the first of 14 vessels of its class.

— *U.S. Coast Guard*

Starting in 1979, the Derecktor Shipyard operated on former Navy property at Coddington Cove. Employment reached 700 before the yard closed about 10 years after opening.

The Honorable Florence K. Murray, of Newport, was named the first woman justice of the Rhode Island Supreme Court. She was sworn in on November 9, 1979.

The 58,000-ton battleship *Iowa* visited Newport for several days in May 1987. She was boarded by countless visitors, who were amused to learn it was the only Navy ship with a bathtub — installed for the convenience of President Franklin D. Roosevelt.

Even if students at St. George's School can't remember the score of a March 1989 basketball game with Middlesex School, they are apt to recall certain statistics of the encounter: 47 personal fouls, two technical fouls and 65 free throws.

Jamestown made state history when it appointed Frances B. Shocket, on September 13, 1992, to be the Town's administrator, the first woman in Rhode Island to serve in that capacity.

On December 3, 1993, Major General James M. Lyle, the commanding general of the U.S. Army Reserve Officer Training Corps (ROTC), commended Rogers High School for its successful recruitment drive. Lyle is a graduate of the school and was once a member of its ROTC program.

On July 27, 1994, the New York Yacht Club announced the International Challenge Cup, an amateur sailing competition to be held in Newport every three years, beginning in 1996.

And, 25 years ago, in 1969, humans landed on the moon. What will the next 25 years bring?

During commissioning ceremonies ▷ on July 9, 1994, members of the *USS Rhode Island*'s crew salute the people of its namesake state.
— *Newport Daily News*

Acknowledgements, Part II

Although the previous pages only review the past 25 years, so much took place that we called upon the assistance of many interested people to determine what was to be recorded, and to check copy in order to maintain accuracy. The author and Bank of Newport's Anniversary Committee thank the following for assistance: Albert K. Sherman, Jr., publisher, and David Offer, editor, of *The Newport Daily News*; David Sanders, public information officer, Naval Education and Training Center; Benjamin Reed, Newport Restoration Foundation; John Pantalone, editor, *Newport This Week*; photographers John T. Hopf and John W. Corbett; Col. Frank Hale, Newport Artillery Company; Dr. A. R. G. Wallace; Officer Michael McKenna, Newport Police Department; Fire Marshal George L. Pennachi, Newport Fire Department; Dr. Daniel Snydacker, Judith Youngken and Bertram Lippincott, Newport Historical Society; Monique M. Panaggio, Preservation Society of Newport County; *The Providence Journal-Bulletin*; Evan Smith, Newport County Convention & Visitors Bureau; John Cronin, director of operations, Economic Innovations Center; Anthony Nicolosi, director, Naval War College Museum; Mark Stenning, International Tennis Hall of Fame; the staff of Redwood Library (in particular, Linda Gordon); the staff of Newport Public Library; Herbert A. Lawton, Jr.; Barclay Douglas, Jr.; Tylor Field; William H. Leys; Patrick O'Neill Hayes; Peter W. Armitage and Donna Amatore of FitzGerald & Company; and particularly to Pamela R. Berger, vice president of marketing, Bank of Newport.

The author thanks the Anniversary Committee of Bank of Newport: Peter S. Damon, president and chief executive officer, Bank of Newport; David P. Leys, chairman, Bank of Newport (and chairman of the Anniversary Committee); John H. Ellis, Charlotte Yeomans and Pamela R. Berger, officers, Bank of Newport; Ellen S. Murphy, corporator, Bank of Newport; and Susan K. McCarthy, FitzGerald & Company.

Bibliography

Bridenbaugh, Carl. *Cities in the Wilderness, The First Century of Urban Life in America 1625-1742*. The Ronald Press Company. New York. 1938.

Browne, Howard S., M.D., F.A.C.S. *The Newport Hospital — A History 1873-1973*. Mowbray Company. Providence. 1976.

Chapin, Howard M. *Documentary History of Newport, Vol. II*. Preston and Rounds Co. Providence. 1919.

Columbia Encyclopedia In One Volume, The. Compiled and Edited at Columbia University, Clarke F. Ansley, editor-in-chief. Columbia University Press. New York. 1935.

Downing, Antoinette F. and Scully, Vincent J., Jr. *The Architectural Heritage of Newport, Rhode Island 1640-1915*. Harvard University Press. Cambridge. 1952.

Early Religious Leaders of Newport. A series of articles by Rev. Franklin G. McKeever, D.D.; Dr. William J. Hull; Rev. Claris Edwin Silcox; Rev. Stanley C. Hughes; Rev. J. Pereira Mendes, D.D.; Rev. William I. Ward; Rev. William Safford Jones; Rev. Roderick Terry, D.D. Published for the Newport Historical Society by Mercury Publishing Co. Newport. 1918.

Elliott, Maud Howe. *This Was My Newport*. The Mythology Company, A. Marshall Jones. Cambridge. 1944.

Encyclopedia of the American Revolution. Mark Mayo Boatner III. David McKay Company, Inc. New York. 1966.

Gentlemen's Progress: The Itinerarium of Dr. Alexander Hamilton 1744. Edited and with an introduction by Carl Bridenbaugh. Published for the Institute of Early American History and Culture at Williamsburg, Virginia, by the University of North Carolina Press. Chapel Hill. 1948.

Jeffreys, C. P. B. *Newport: A Short History*. Newport Historical Society. Newport. 1992.

Mason, George Champlin. *Reminiscences of Newport*. Charles E. Hammett, Jr. Newport. 1884.

McAdam, Roger Williams. *Commonwealth, Giantess of the Sound*. Stephen Daye Press. New York. 1959.

Pell, Claiborne deB. *Rochambeau and Rhode Island*. State of Rhode Island and Providence Plantations. General Rochambeau Commission. (n.d.; n.p.)

Records of the Colony of Rhode Island and Providence Plantations. 10 Volumes, 1636-1792. John Russell Bartlett, Secretary of State. A. Crawford Greene and Brother, State Printers. Providence. Published from mid-1850s to mid-1860s.

Rhode Island: A Guide to the Smallest State. American Guide Series; written by workers of the Works Progress Administration for the State of Rhode Island; sponsored by Louis W. Cappelli, Secretary of State, Chairman of the Sponsoring Committee. The Riverside Press. Cambridge. 1937.

Richards, J(ohn) J. *Rhode Island's Early Defenders and Their Successors*. Rhode Island Pendulum. East Greenwich, R.I. 1937.

Taverner, Gilbert Y. *St. George's School — A History: 1896-1986*. Reynolds-DeWalt Printing, Inc. New Bedford. 1987.

Miscellaneous Information Sources:
Jamestown Press
Newport Social Index (various annual editions)
Newport City Directories (various annual editions)
Newport Daily News
Newport Herald
Newport Mercury
Newport Navalog
Newport This Week
Providence Journal-Bulletin
Providence Journal Almanac
Sakonnet Times

Index

Illustrations and photographs are indicated by boldface numerals.

Notes

About the Author

Leonard J. Panaggio is eminently qualified to write a book about his native city. He was the editor and publisher of *Newport Topic*, a weekly newspaper, and formerly was on the staff of the Newport Historical Society. From 1948 to 1952, he served as the first director of public relations for Old Sturbridge Village, in Massachusetts. He returned to Rhode Island, in 1952, to  serve as the State's first director of tourist promotion, a position he held until he retired in 1983.

John W. Corbett

He is a member of several professional organizations, including the Society of American Travel Writers, and the Rhode Island Press Association — for which he has served as president. He is a member of the Rhode Island State Records Advisory Commission, and is affiliated with several historical societies and preservation groups in several states.

During his career with the State of Rhode Island, he served as secretary of the State's Civil War Centennial Commission, and as secretary of its Heritage Month Committee. Mr. Panaggio was the press officer for the America's Cup races, from the time the series was revived, in 1958, until 1983; he also worked in the same capacity for "Tall Ships '76." He was a member of the Coordinating Committee of the U.S. National Parks Service and was also on President Johnson's "Discover America" Task Force.

Mr. Panaggio is a columnist for the *Newport Daily News* and a travel writer for *Newport This Week*. He contributes articles to "Sea Classics" magazine.

An Air Force veteran with three years of World War II service in North Africa, he is married to the former Monique Rouger. She is director of public relations for the Preservation Society of Newport County. They have a son and a daughter.

Portrait of Newport II

Book design and typesetting by Peter Armitage,
cover design by Paul Brennan, FitzGerald & Company.
Composed in Centaur and Syntax, using QuarkXPress.
Printed by Meridien Printing on Finch Opaque.
Bound in King James.